Guide to Martha's Vineyard

Praise for previous editions:

"Essential for tourists and first-time visitors as well as a useful tool for those more familiar with our island."

—The *Vineyard Gazette*

"As the guide is written by a long-time resident familiar with the history and offerings of Martha's Vineyard, the visitor is afforded an insider's experiences and suggestions on how to organize a trip based on a combination of the island's offerings and one's budget."

—The *Midwest Book Review*

"Practical as well as lyrical . . . this is a good basic guidebook."

—The *Providence Sunday Journal*

"In providing this comprehensive guide, the author has done her part to make people aware of this remarkable place."

—*Sunday Cape Cod Times*

"Polly Burroughs advis[es] visitors about both the natural beauties and social scene to be enjoyed on the famous island."

—*Blâde Citizen* (Oceanside, Calif.)

Help Us Keep This Guide Up to Date

Every effort has been made by the author and editors to make this guide as accurate and useful as possible. However, many things can change after a guide is published—establishments close, phone numbers change, facilities come under new management, and so on.

We would love to hear from you concerning your experiences with this guide and how you feel it could be made better and be kept up to date. While we may not be able to respond to all comments and suggestions, we'll take them to heart and we'll also make certain to share them with the author. Please send your comments and suggestions to the following address:

The Globe Pequot Press
Reader Response/Editorial Department
P.O. Box 480
Guilford, CT 06437

Or you may e-mail us at:
editorial@globe-pequot.com

Thanks for the input, and happy travels!

pas possible, cet enfant. Je prenais pourtant mes précautions. Peut-être que j'ai oublié quelques fois? Je ne sais plus. Je touche mon ventre, incrédule; il est encore tout plat. En même temps, je me sens si forte, tout à coup : je porte un enfant, je porte la vie. J'avais dit à André que je vivrais pour deux, eh bien! voilà! Mais Georg, comment va-t-il accueillir la nouvelle? Va-t-il m'en vouloir? Va-t-il reconnaître sa paternité, ou laisser mon bébé orphelin? Je sais bien qu'il veut des enfants, mais, là, comme ça, sans que nous ayons vécu ensemble, avec l'Atlantique entre nous?

Comment vais-je arriver à élever cet enfant toute seule et à poursuivre mon travail qui me prend tellement de temps? Je ne pourrais pas être une mère seule et travailler soixante heures par semaine. Non, ce ne serait pas possible… Je serais une mère trop absente et, comme le père est si loin, il n'y aurait que des étrangers pour s'occuper de notre enfant. Peut-être qu'il serait malheureux. Peut-être qu'il vaudrait mieux ne pas le mettre au monde.

Pourtant, petit, je t'aimerais tant! Tu es déjà la petite vie qu'Anna voyait dans la mienne, le présage des jours de bonheur qu'elle entrevoyait pour moi quand j'arpentais les corridors les plus sombres de mon existence.

*

Un jour, je veux avoir mon enfant quoi qu'il advienne. Le jour d'après, l'accueillir me semble impossible. Peut-être que je m'en fais trop. Peut-être que, si on réfléchit trop, on ne fait jamais rien. Peut-être que, si on attend le moment parfait, on passe à côté de tout ce qui compte. Et qu'est-ce qui compte, justement? Vivre. Aimer. Donner. C'est tellement cliché! Mais, si c'est cliché, c'est parce que c'est vrai.

Je pourrais aller rejoindre Georg à Oslo comme nous l'avons évoqué récemment. Mais c'est complètement fou! Il me faudrait tout laisser derrière moi. Quoique je pourrais prendre deux ans de congé sans solde, ce qui limiterait les risques côté carrière en attendant de voir comment je peux m'intégrer en Norvège.

Sinon, quel choix me reste-t-il? Me faire avorter, pleurer une autre mort, une autre séparation? Laisser la raison tuer les sentiments?

Je réfléchis seule, sans en parler à Georg. Il lui appartient aussi de réfléchir à notre avenir, mais je dois d'abord voir clair en moi avant d'aborder le sujet avec lui. J'ai l'impression de mentir en ne lui disant pas tout, mais il me faut un peu de temps pour accueillir l'imprévu. On remplit le présent à échafauder des plans que la vie semble s'amuser à détourner.

*

Une nuit, un cauchemar me réveille en sursaut. Je suis couverte de sueur. J'allume la lumière et revois comme dans le mauvais rêve un petit enfant tombant dans le vide, du haut de mon balcon qui semble situé au cent dixième étage d'une tour. C'est une vision affolante, terrifiante, et pourtant éclairante. J'ai besoin de parler à Georg tout de suite.

— Georg, c'est Satie.

— Satie, ma chérie, comme je suis content de te parler! Tu me manques terriblement. Je suis content d'entendre ta voix. Je ne m'y attendais pas si tard dans ta nuit.

— Je suis désolée de t'appeler à l'heure où tu dois partir travailler.

— Non, ne le sois pas. Je t'ai toujours dit que tu pouvais m'appeler n'importe quand et j'aime que tu sois là au moment où je vais commencer ma journée.

— Je ne suis pas certaine que tu pourras te concentrer sur ton travail après ce que je vais te dire…

— Que se passe-t-il? Ça ne va pas? Tu as des problèmes?

— Georg… j'attends un enfant de toi et…

Silence étonné, suivi d'une explosion de joie au bout du fil. J'aimerais voir le visage heureux de mon bel amour, mais, en pleine nuit, le téléphone s'imposait devant Skype.

— Satie, tu vas le garder? demande-t-il, quand l'inquiétude prend le pas sur la gaîté.

— Ça m'est impossible de ne pas accueillir la vie. Tu veux bien de nous deux chez toi? dis-je avec un sourire dans la voix.

— Prenez le premier avion que je vous embrasse, toi et ton ventre!

— Georg…

— Oui…

— Je t'aime!

*

Quatre énormes valises à traîner et sept heures d'avion jusqu'à Georg après les au revoir à la famille et aux amis qui sont encore sous le choc de mon départ. Mais, moi, maintenant, je ressens l'urgence de vivre. L'urgence d'aimer.

Adieu, André. Adieu, chansons tristes. Sept heures d'avion avec, en boucles dans mes oreilles, un de ces refrains euphorisants d'Indochine. *Moi je veux vivre, vivre, vivre, encore plus fort!*

Et danser ma vie. À trois dans quelques mois.

GUIDE TO MARTHA'S VINEYARD

Eighth Edition

by
Polly Burroughs

Photographs by Mike Wallo

Guilford, Connecticut

The prices and rates in this guide were confirmed at press time. We recommend, however, that you call establishments to obtain current information before traveling.

Cover photo by Craig R. Dripps
Cover design by Saralyn D'Amato-Twomey
Text design by Deborah Nicolais

Library of Congress Cataloging-in-Publication Data

Burroughs, Polly.
Guide to Martha's Vineyard / by Polly Burroughs. – 8th ed.
p. cm.
Includes index.
ISBN 0-7627-0432-2
1. Martha's Vineyard (Mass.)–Guidebooks. I. Title.
F72.M5B875 1999
917.44'94–dc21 98-48364
CIP

Manufactured in the United States of America
Eighth Edition/Second Printing

Acknowledgments

The author is indebted to the following individuals for their generous assistance in helping to put together this guide: Art Railton, former President of the Vineyard Museum; Richard Reston, Publisher and General Manager of the *Vineyard Gazette,* for use of the paper's superb archives; Mike Wallo, Production Manager of the *Gazette,* for his excellent photography.

I would also like to thank Linda Kennedy, President of the Globe Pequot Press, who made it all possible, and my editor Elizabeth Taylor for her valuable help with this edition, the guide's twentieth year of continuous publication.

All selections of lodgings and restaurants have been made by the author. *No one can pay or is paid to be in this book.*

Contents

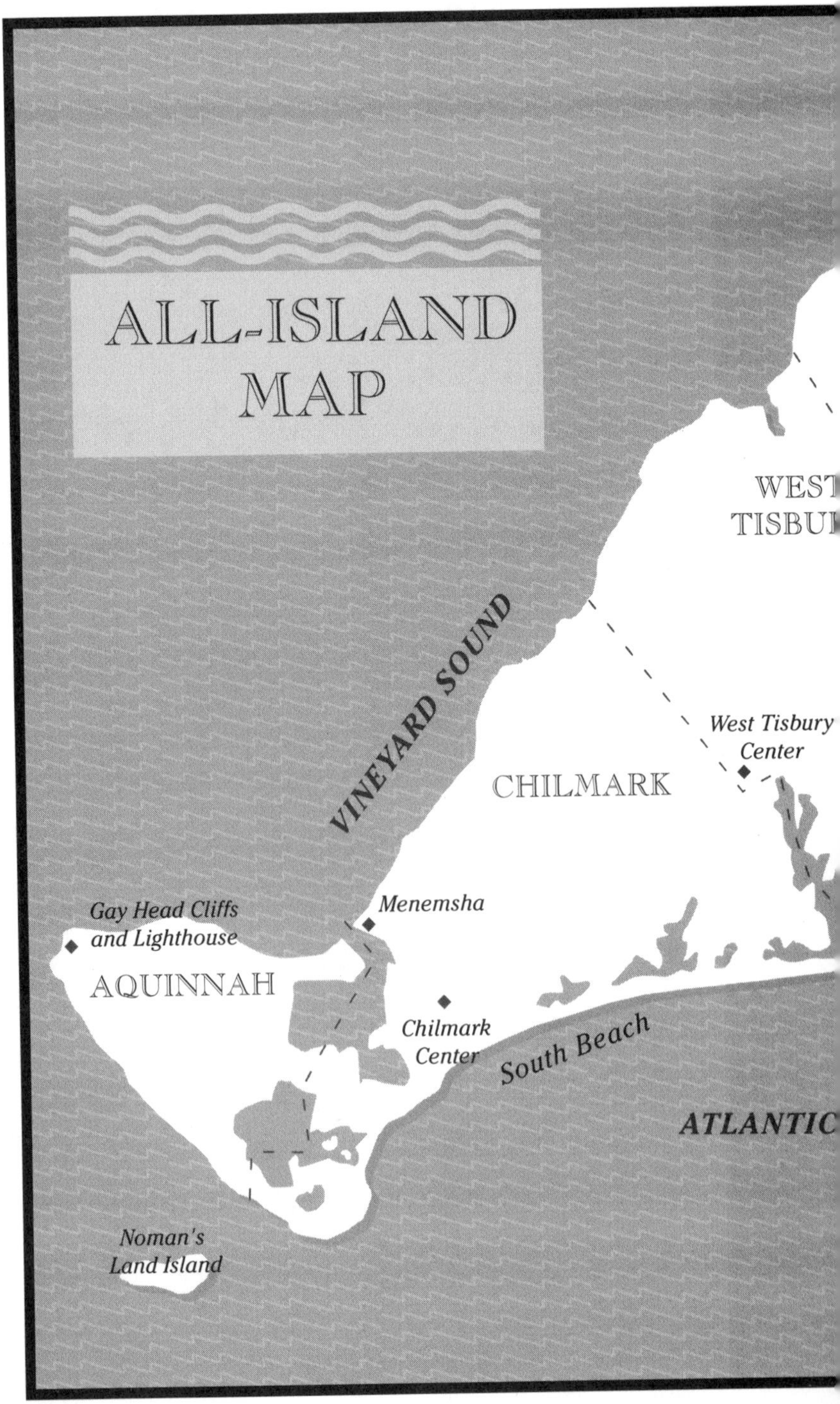

ALL-ISLAND MAP

WEST
TISBU

VINEYARD SOUND

West Tisbury
Center

CHILMARK

Menemsha

Gay Head Cliffs
and Lighthouse

AQUINNAH

Chilmark
Center

South Beach

ATLANTIC

Noman's
Land Island

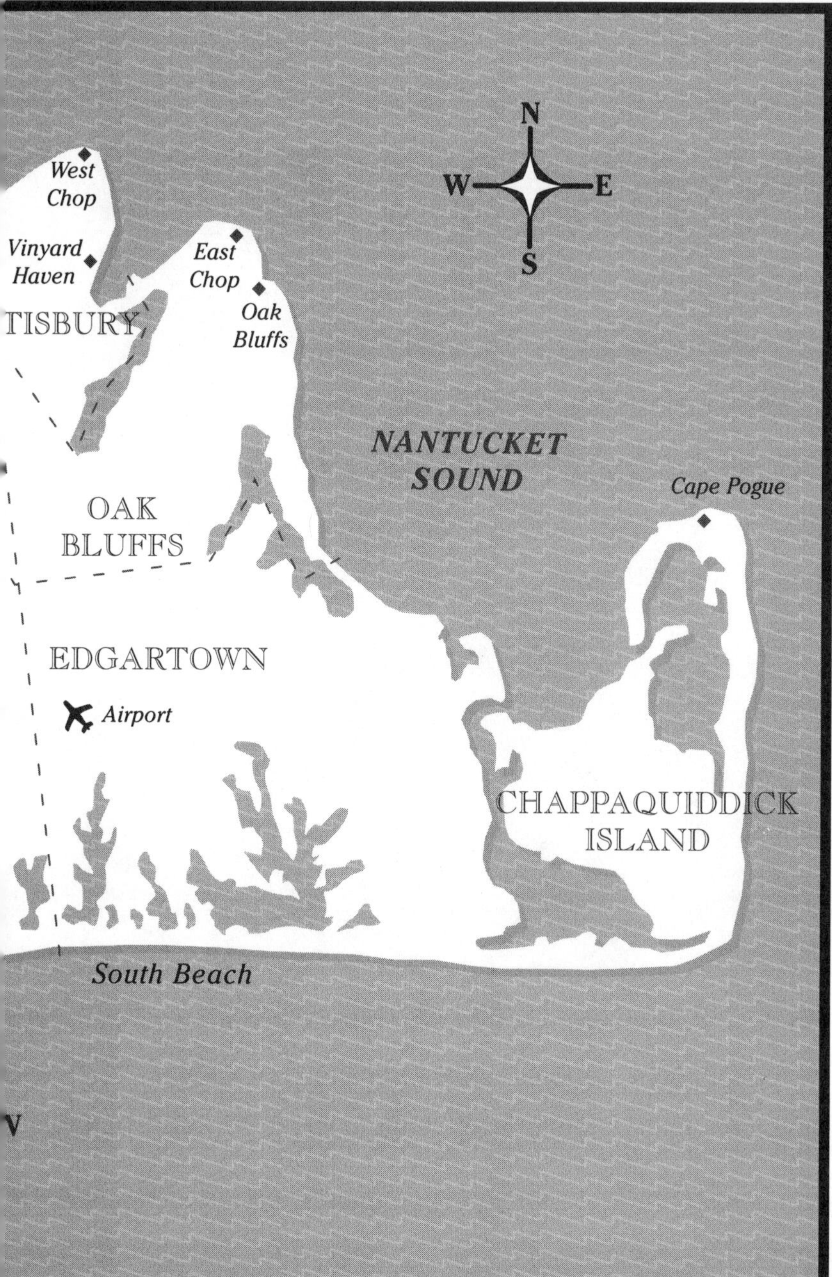

N
W
E
S
West Chop
Vinyard Haven
East Chop
Oak Bluffs
TISBURY
OAK BLUFFS
NANTUCKET SOUND
Cape Pogue
EDGARTOWN
Airport
CHAPPAQUIDDICK ISLAND
South Beach

V

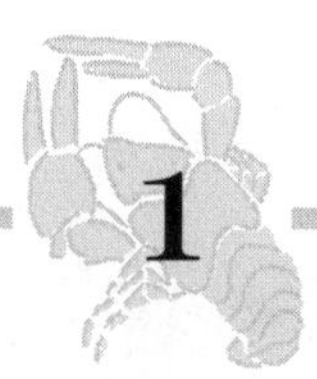

1

The Island's Profile

The island of Martha's Vineyard lies 5 miles off the shoulder of Cape Cod. Twenty miles long and 9 miles wide at its broadest point, the island is triangular and encircled by the Vineyard Sound, the Nantucket Sound, and the Atlantic Ocean. With hills, valleys, and flat plains, the island is as renowned for the beauty of its varied geological landscape as it is for the individual character of its six towns.

A boulder-strewn ridge runs all along the north shore of the island, extending to the high, rolling moors at the island's western tip. The wooded, mid-island outwash plains, which were formed by the waters that flowed from melting glacial ice, reach down to the windswept beaches along the south shore, where fingerlike ponds jut in from the ocean. Estuaries rich with marine and bird life fringe the island's shores. Four superb harbors are sculpted into the Vineyard and Nantucket Sound side of the island. From the beginning of time, the sea and winds have shaped and reshaped these contours, just as they have helped shape the island's human history since the arrival of the first permanent white settlers in 1642.

Of all the island's assets, the sea and the ocean beaches are the great attraction for vacationers. Once the artery for America's founding and development, and to the Vineyarders their livelihood and only means of communication with the outside world, the sea has once again given the island its economic base by attracting thousands of vacationers each summer. It is an extremely popular summer resort. The number of hotels, inns, guest houses, restaurants, and stores, as well as the variety of concerts, lectures, fairs, sports, walking tours, auctions, performing arts, and other activities for the visitor, has increased dramatically in the past ten years. While the winter population of 14,000 has increased slowly through the years, the summer influx of vacationers quickly escalates to 85,000 by early July, not counting the day-trippers who come over on cruise ships to visit the island or those in hotels and inns.

To cope with the burgeoning number of visitors each summer, certain changes have been made. There are many more ferries running than in the past; shuttle buses serve all of the towns; free parking arrangements have been made to cope with traffic congestion; and many more places to stay, eat, shop, and rent cars and bikes have become available to the public. And yet not everything has changed, for standards to preserve the scenic beauty of the island continue as they have for years. There are no bathhouses or food stands at any of the beaches; there are still no traffic lights on the island; and signs at many beaches and wildlife sanctuaries warn visitors not to disturb bird nesting areas, trample or drive on the dunes, or leave litter.

Despite the growth of the island population, tradition runs deep in all six towns. Evidence of their Yankee heritage is most apparent in the off-season, when the population dwindles. The pace slackens, and islanders settle down to small-town life with its small-town rhythms.

The six towns are as well known for their individuality as were the early Yankees, whose independent character and idiosyncrasies are legendary. Certain customs have prevailed, and one is the usage of the terms *Up-Island* and *Down-Island,* which are important for the newcomer to understand.

When a ship sails in an easterly direction, it is decreasing or running "down" the degrees of longitude toward zero at Greenwich, England. A westbound vessel, on the other hand, is running "up" its longitude. Thus the Down-Island towns are those on the eastern and northeastern ends of the island: Vineyard Haven, Oak Bluffs, Edgartown, and the island of Chappaquiddick. The Up-Island communities include North and West Tisbury (which are geographically in mid-island, but considered Up-Island), and Chilmark and Gay Head, which is now called Aquinnah, at the westernmost tip. A ship moving through Vineyard Sound sails "up" to New York and "down" east to Maine.

The island's principal port of entry and bustling commercial center is Vineyard Haven, whose maritime origins are rooted in coastal shipping. The town's residential areas have

On Memorial Day children toss flowers into the harbor in memory of the men lost at sea in Edgartown, Oak Bluffs, and Vineyard Haven.

more year-round homes than are found elsewhere on the island. There are some attractive and quiet places to stay a few blocks from the center, and the visitor will find good restaurants, attractive gift shops, and bike, moped, car, and boat rentals readily available. Although the town does have two small beaches, vacationers will probably want to use the big public beaches elsewhere on the island. Public tennis is available in town and golf in nearby West Chop. Evenings are quiet because the town does not have a liquor license, but there are many things to do: movies, theater, the lectures and courses sponsored throughout the year by the Nathan Mayhew Seminars, year-round entertainment at the Katherine Cornell Theatre, and the very popular Wintertide Coffee House. Some of the inn and motel prices are a bit more modest than most places in Edgartown.

The Down-Island town of Oak Bluffs first became popular as a Methodist camp meeting place in the mid-nineteenth century and soon after became a very large summer resort, which it still is. It no longer has huge hotels (nearly all of them were destroyed by fire), but the summer frivolity and seaside boardwalk atmosphere prevail, along with its extraordinary Carpenter Gothic architecture. A merry-go-round, pizza and ice cream parlors, saltwater taffy stands, and shops cater to the tourists from the excursion boats running back and forth to the Cape Cod towns of Falmouth and Hyannis. The town's U-shaped harbor

The Allen Sheep Farm reaches down to the sea. The wool that is sheared here is used for sweaters and blankets sold on the farm.

is jammed with powerboats, and a very attractive sandy beach runs along either side of the ferry dock. There are public tennis courts and a golf course. The rates for rooms in Oak Bluffs, which aren't too fancy, are less than those at other places on the island.

The visual character of Edgartown evolved from whaling-industry money made during the nineteenth century. With its handsome architecture, brick sidewalks, fences ablaze with roses, and beautiful gardens, it is the prettiest town on the island. Flags fly everywhere in Edgartown, another reminder of its maritime background. The majority of the Vineyard's hotels and inns are clustered in the village proper, where there's an endless array of restaurants, gift shops, boutiques, boat rentals, sailboat charters, the island's performing arts center, and one beach, all within walking distance. There are public tennis courts and two large public beaches within 3 miles of the center of town, and another beach and wildlife reservation on Chappaquiddick Island, a distance of 3 miles

Do's and Don'ts

DO pay attention to the posted rules and regulations at all beaches.

DO use bicycle paths if you are bicycling.

DO have the proper light and reflectors when bicycling at night.

DO watch out for one-way streets in the towns. The streets were laid out in the nineteenth century, and the narrow ones in the center of all three Down-Island towns are one-way.

DO keep your voice down in the towns during the evening hours. No shouting! This has become a serious problem.

DO be courteous to others.

DO be responsible for your own trash.

DO keep your dog on a leash at all times when in public, and keep your cat confined to your property, out of consideration for others.

DO pay attention to ocean-swimming conditions and information about Lyme disease.

DON'T drive on any dunes, or trample them, or harm the vegetation.

DON'T pick any wildflowers.

DON'T disturb any small clams, scallops, or other shellfish.

DON'T bicycle on the sidewalks.

DON'T wear bathing suits in the center of the towns or appear shirtless or barefoot. Rollerblades and bikes are not allowed in the centers of any towns.

DON'T leave any litter on any street, beach, or roadway.

DON'T sleep in your car or on the beach anywhere on the island. It is illegal.

DON'T drive over 45 miles per hour; the speed limit is even slower on most roads.

DON'T dump any boat sewage into the harbors. There is a heavy fine.

The Island Idiom

The Island idiom, that wonderful, illogical way of explaining and expressing things is disappearing on the island. But there are still some around who speak in their unique way and are—inadvertently—very funny.

An old mason had been working on a large field stone chimney. One morning, after an hour or so, he just picked up his tools, put them in his truck, and started to leave. "Why are you leaving?" his puzzled employer asked. "Them stones ain't talkin' to me today," he muttered and got in his truck and drove off.

One summer resident ordered a new stove unit to be installed during the winter. She arrived in June for the summer to discover nothing had been done.

"Why didn't you call me?" she asked the appliance man.

"Why should I," he replied, "They didn't have it."

The Edgartown shipyard has a fine trailer for hauling boats in and out of the harbor. The truck to which it's attached is, of course, called The Happy Hooker.

from the island's ferry. The town has become very congested in the summertime, so free parking lots outside of town and a shuttle bus service have been introduced.

To stay Up-Island, a car is a necessity, as it may be a 5- or 6-mile drive to a beach or a grocery store. With its many sparsely settled areas, it is very rural and quiet. West and North Tisbury, which cut across the middle of the island from shore to shore, have very little beach access, and West Tisbury's center seems more like a New England farming community than does any other place on the island. It has always been a farming community; the annual country fair is here, and there are several riding stables. The new Agricultural Hall in the center of town is used for various events, and there are lectures and musical programs at the Congregational Church. There are a few places to stay, but most visitors rent private homes or beach cottages.

With its high, rolling hills and sweeping views of the Atlantic Ocean and Vineyard Sound, the Up-Island town of Chilmark is very beautiful. In recent years its land has become some of the most expensive on the island. Chilmark has no private clubs, but the community center is a gathering place for residents and visitors where there are sports—baseball, tennis, but no golf—lectures, concerts, nature walks, and programs for children. Chilmark Center, called Beetlebung Corner, has a summer grocer, a very good restaurant, and a couple of shops, while Chilmark's fishing port of Menemsha has its own beach, several eating places, a couple of gift and clothing shops, a gas station, a grocer, a post office, and two fish markets. The picturesque harbor is small and crowded with fishing and pleasure boats. There are several places to stay in Chilmark; in addition, private homes can be rented.

Island of Everyman

There are many celebrities on the Island and some don't realize they won't be treated any differently than anyone else and learn the hard way.

One very well-known cabinet officer from Washington wanted a hardware store order delivered that afternoon. "We deliver on Thursday," the clerk replied, writing up the order.

"But you don't know who I am," he explained, going to great length to describe his important position.

Ignoring the gentleman's comments, the clerk continued to write out the sales slip.

"We deliver on Thursday."

It was a quiet, windless Sunday afternoon in the 1960s and there were very few boats in Edgartown Harbor. A large motorboat eased in toward the shipyard and a voice boomed out, "My name is Senator Javits. We'd like dockage space." Dead silence. Then a voice boomed back, "My name is Leon Estabrook. There ain't none."

Children playing at Wompanaug

The Indian town of Aquinnah on the western tip of the island is a premier tourist attraction because of the Gay Head Cliffs. The cliffs have a very fine restaurant, take-out food stands, and a cluster of tourist gift shops that cater to busloads of sightseers. There are few places to stay in the town other than private home rentals.

Wherever you decide to stay on the Vineyard, you'll find each town has its individual character emanating from its historic roots. The scope of things to do and the variety of places to go in each town have fascinated and delighted visitors since the nineteenth century.

Looking "over Jordan" to the hotel and Camp Grounds in Oak Bluffs.
(COURTESY OF THE VINEYARD MUSEUM)

2

A Brief History

There have been many theories and much speculation about early explorers landing on Nantucket, Martha's Vineyard, and Cape Cod, but the first written observations about the Vineyard were made by the Reverend John Brereton and Gabriel Archer, who sailed from England to these shores in 1602 aboard Captain Bartholomew Gosnold's ship. According to their reports and the authoritative research by two prominent English historians, David and Allison Quinn (published by the Hakluyt Society in London in 1983), they made their first landfall on Cape Pogue on Chappaquiddick. The Quinns noted, "the probability that it is Gosnold's first [sighting of] Martha's Vineyard is very high indeed."

They went ashore, and Brereton noted in his report: "Going around about it, we found it to be foure English miles in compasse without house or inhabitant." Both men were impressed by the vegetation and berries; the strawberries were "bigger than ours in England," and bushes—raspberries, blueberries, huckleberries, and grapevines—were familiar. Brereton continued, "Such an incredible store of vines, as well in the woodie part of the Island where they run vpon every tree, as on the outward parts, that we could not goe for treading vpon them." They were equally impressed with the ducks, geese, and other wildfowl, the beach peas growing on the sandy shore, and "huge bones and ribbes of whale." Archer wrote of similar impressions, but also stated, "We named it Martha's Vineyard," which historians believe was for Gosnold's daughter Martha and possibly for his mother-in-law, Martha Golding. The Vineyard part of the name came from the masses of grapevines they saw everywhere.

The vessel moved on to the main island, where they encountered American Indians (they had only seen evidence of inhabitants on Chappaquiddick). Brereton wrote: "Yet we found no townes, nor many of their houses, although we saw manie Indians, which are tall, big boned men, all naked, sauing they couer their priuy parts with a blacke tewed skin, much like a Black-smiths apron, tied about their middle and betweene their legs behinde: they gaue vs their fish readie boiled, (which they carried in a basket made of twigges)," and shared their tobacco, which they smoked in pipes made of hard, dry clay. The Indian name for the island was Noepe, meaning "amid the waters."

These Indians were of the Pokanocket Confederacy, who inhabited the surrounding islands as well. Also called Wampanoags, meaning "Easterners," they belonged to the Algonquian linguistic group, which extended in a great semicircle from the Carolinas up into Canada and west to the Rocky Mountains. At the time the Pilgrims landed, Massasoit was the sachem, or chief, of the Algonquian Confederation.

Whaling was Edgartown's principal industry in the nineteenth century.

The paddle-wheel steamer Martha's Vineyard *leaves Oak Bluffs while vacationers wave from their catboats.* (Photographs Courtesy of the Vineyard Museum)

Gosnold weighed anchor and sailed up Vineyard Sound to Cuttyhunk Island, the outermost in the Elizabeth Island chain that stretches out from Woods Hole. They stayed most of the summer here and loaded their vessel with sassafras root, skins, and furs bartered from the friendly Indians before they returned to England.

It was forty years later, in 1641, that Thomas Mayhew of Watertown, Massachusetts, purchased for forty pounds the Vineyard, Nantucket, and the Elizabeth Islands from two English noblemen who held conflicting grants to the area. The following year his son, Thomas Mayhew, Jr., arrived with a group and chose Edgartown for the island's first white settlement. They called it Great Harbor. The town's official name was bestowed by Governor Lovelace of New York in 1671 (when Martha's Vineyard was for a time part of New York) in honor of Edgar, infant son of the Duke of York, heir apparent to the British crown. Both Dutchess County and Queens County in New York were named at the same time. The town subsequently became the county seat for the Vineyard and the Elizabeth Islands.

These first settlers found the Indians to be a handsome, disciplined, and peaceful tribe, as Brereton had noted. The Indians' economy was based on fishing and farming, rather than hunting, and they willingly shared their knowledge of taming the wilderness, whaling alongshore, gathering fruit and shellfish, seining the creeks for herring in the spring, catching cod and eel in the winter, hunting wild game, and planting corn in the spring. Thomas Mayhew began his work to Christianize the friendly Indians, and the little settlement grew very slowly. (There were about eighty-five white people on the island in 1660.) Fifteen years later his son was the first of many islanders to perish at sea. Thomas Mayhew, Jr., had left Boston on a mission to England, and his vessel was never heard from again.

His father continued to Christianize the Indians, as did three succeeding generations, earning themselves the name "Missionary Mayhews." They exercised an important influence over the island's growth and character. There was never open hostility between these settlers and the natives, although Governor Mayhew's authority as chief magistrate was eventually challenged by other settlers, who accused the

Mayhews of running a feudal state. As time passed, natives were edged off the richer lands on the island; the white settlers did, however, purchase these lands, not confiscate them. Some Indians moved off the island to the mainland, and others moved to Chappaquiddick or to Aquinnah, which is now one of the two Indian townships in the state.

By tradition, these early English settlers were farmers, and gradually settlements other than Edgartown took root on the island. They became almost totally self-sufficient fishing and farming communities where boats and fishing gear were used equally with plows, wagons, and harrows. Not only were pigs, chickens, and cows in the barnyard, but great flocks of sheep roamed the moors. There were mills along the north shore to grind corn and make brick and paint from clay. Vineyarders

Missouri muralist Thomas Hart Benton, a lifelong summer resident of Martha's Vineyard, rendered this painting of his Chilmark neighbor Josie West, a deaf mute farmer. Despite his handicaps, West supported himself by selling butter, eggs, milk, and mutton to summer visitors. An expert woodsman, he also sold firewood.

(Courtesy of the Vineyard Museum)

Zeb Tilton

There were many famous seamen in the Vineyard's long maritime history. The most unforgettable character who became a legend in his time was Captain Zebulon Northrop Tilton, the Paul Bunyan of the coast-wise schooner trade.

Zeb was known in every port from South Street to Maine, where he moved freight under canvas for half a century. Born in 1867, he was a huge, skilled seaman, and it was said he could sail to Chicago in a heavy dew. His celebrated life afloat and ashore, and his love of women and colorful wit attracted a gathering wherever he put into port. He said he knew the coast so well that he could tell where he was when the fog was as thick as cotton batting by tasting the water. When he decided on his third wife he said, "She's got all her teeth and not a grey hair in her head . . ." So he and Grace McDonald did get married in New Bedford and sailed off with a load of freight.

The stories about Zeb and his extraordinary career live on—and though he was too plain a figure for fancy words, he was indeed a "stronger and braver Cyrano, a wittier and leaner Falstaff."

wove their own cloth from the sheep's wool, evaporated the sea water for salt, hunted wild game, grew their own vegetables, and fashioned their farm tools on anvils.

From the earliest times Vineyarders also looked to the sea and maritime trade for their livelihood. They exported cranberries, wool, candles, whale oil, and salt cod, which, with New England rum, were the basis of Yankee trade with the Catholic countries of Europe as well as the Azores, the Cape Verde Islands, and the West Indies. The growth of Vineyard Haven was directly proportionate to the expansion of maritime trade between the American colonies and the West Indies, as the town became a primary anchorage for vessels moving up and down the coast.

Whaling became Edgartown's principal industry. Although sheep farming on the island was successful, it was the sea, with its possibilities for adventure and profit, that lured man and boy down to the waterfront. For over two centuries the

Captain Zeb Tilton aboard his coast-wise schooner, the Alice S. Wentworth.

majority of Vineyard men earned their living as fishermen, merchant seamen, whalers, or pilots, sailing aboard barks, packets, coast-wise schooners, sloops, and even clipper ships.

Edgartown and Vineyard Haven reached the peak of their prosperity in the nineteenth century. By 1914 the completion of the Cape Cod Canal and the increased movement of freight by steamship, train, and truck, rather than under sail, signaled the decline of Vineyard Haven's busy port. In addition, the discovery of petroleum in 1859 had undercut the whaling industry, whose end was hastened by the loss of Yankee ships during the Civil War; by World War I the industry was finished.

Changes came slowly, but they were irreversible. Oak Bluffs came into being as a popular Methodist camp meeting place in 1835, and eventually it became the island's first summer resort. The resort business became increasingly important through the years and has now replaced everything else and become the island's primary source of income. Despite all the changes, the towns have continued to retain their individual characters: Edgartown with its handsome whaling captains' houses and stately elms; the summer holiday frivolity of Oak Bluffs' gingerbread architecture; Vineyard Haven, the island's commercial center; the farming community of West Tisbury, whose agricultural origins are still strong and seem far from the sea; the meeting of sea and soil in Chilmark, where gray, weathered farmhouses dot the rolling moors; Gay Head, now called Acquinnah, is still an Indian township; and Menemsha, which is the last true fishing village on the island.

3

When to Go

Martha's Vineyard has four distinct seasons for the visitor to consider, and, of course, summer is the most popular season. The weather is very pleasant; with the prevailing southwest winds, the air temperature averages seventy degrees. On clear, brilliant days the sky is a radiant blue and the sea is a collage of vivid blues and greens. The island's many beaches are crowded with people tanning, playing in the sand, or swimming in the gentle waters of the sound or the rolling surf along the south shore. The warm Gulf Stream offshore and the surrounding sandy shoals, which the sun warms more easily than deep water, cause the water temperature to range from the sixties to the low seventies.

At other times a smoky southwester blows all day, or a fog rolls in from offshore, misting the abundant, breathtaking roses and cloaking the harbors and beaches in muffled stillness. A mournful moan of a foghorn drones, and all boating traffic stays in port. On these days the towns are jammed as crowds flock in to shop, eat, or visit the museums and art galleries.

All summer long there is a wide variety of entertainment nightly, and the typical summer resort activities are available during the day. There's also a constant flow of special events during July and August—house tours, auctions, art shows, parades, celebrations, festivals, fireworks, sailing regattas, road races, and a county fair.

This very busy holiday season slows down on Labor Day with an enormous exodus of visitors. Many people still come to the island through the early fall, but nowhere does it seem crowded. The wonderful weather lingers for weeks, because of the surrounding sound and ocean, which are slow to cool off. During those beautiful September and October days, when the water is still warm enough for hardy swimmers, a yellow haze hangs over the moors in the mornings, the middays are filled with a false warmth, and the evenings are cool.

The still autumn nights are beautiful; the towns are quiet, and a harvest moon casts its glow across the still harbors, silhouetting the few ships riding at anchor.

Out on the beaches at this time of year, the beach plums have turned a succulent purple, the marsh grasses fringing the tidal ponds and the highbush blueberry turn a palette of fall colors, and purple asters and goldenrod blanket the fields Up-Island. The Beetlebung trees turn a brilliant red at Beetlebung Corner. The seaweed also has shed its summer growth. The shallow waters are crystal clear, and the slanting sun sparkles on the water like crumpled tinfoil. The ponds are filled with migrating birds stopping to rest and feed. Summer residents are closing up their houses and cottages all through the fall. Shipyard workers are hauling and storing boats everywhere. Scallopers are busy launching their small workboats before October, when they start dragging for the succulent bivalve that is such an important part of the winter economy.

For the visitor at this halcyon time of year, most of the shops and restaurants are open, although some have limited hours. One big fall attraction is the Fishing Derby from mid-September to mid-October. Tivoli Day in Oak Bluffs includes bicycle races and a street fair as well as several handcraft fairs. Aside from these two major scheduled events, there are many things for the visitor to do (see Chapter 10, Annual Special Events). There are nature walks, bird walks, sports from golf and tennis to horseback riding on the beach, movies, and occasional lectures and concerts. Picnicking on the beach at this time of year, tucked behind a dune if the wind comes up, can be delightful.

By late fall fewer restaurants and shops are open, but those that are gear up for the popular Thanksgiving Weekend. The inns are full, ferries are sold out on certain dates, private homes are reopened, and shops are brimming with Christmas gifts for visitors.

By now the Up-Island towns are very sparsely populated, while the Down-Island towns, which relate much more closely to the mainland, begin to prepare for the Christmas holiday. All through the fall many residents, young and old, have been working at various handcrafts and making jams and jellies in preparation for the Christmas season. By mid-December the handsome, white whaling captains' houses and beautiful churches are decorated with the traditional holly and greens.

Edgartown's Main Street is lined with small Christmas trees running down to the waterfront where the fishing fleet comes in from offshore for the holiday. The second weekend in December, Edgartown has a special "Christmas in Edgartown" celebration, and many of the inns offer reduced rates for the weekend. For the visitor there are walking tours of the historic houses, holiday shopping, carols ringing out from the St. Andrew's Episcopal Church belfry, horse-drawn carriage rides around town, Christmas concerts at the Old Whaling Church, and a parade. Vineyard Haven has its "Twelve Days of Christmas," with Santa arriving on the ferry.

Winter on the Vineyard is very quiet, and the weather is usually moderate, with an average temperature of thirty degrees. Snow lasts only a few days, but the dampness can be penetrating. Bone-chilling raw winds sweep across the empty beaches, and northeasters—sometimes as severe as a hurricane—batter the island and delay the ferries. Occasionally the harbors freeze over.

Even so, the winter population has increased in recent years. Both retired people and young men and women do handcrafts, art, carpentry, boatbuilding, and other occupations through this quiet season. There are winter activities for

Harvesting the hay in West Tisbury.

A summer's day on the south shore.

The Island looks completely different dressed in winter white.

these residents and any visitors: a mid-island ice-skating rink, several health spas, an amateur theater group, indoor tennis, an indoor pool at the high school, special programs at the Old Whaling Church, the Wintertide Coffee House, the Atlantic Connection, the Katherine Cornell Theatre, and a selection of lectures and courses at the Nathan Mayhew Seminars. Cross-country skiing on the beach and dunes is a special treat for as long as the snow lasts.

The ocean is slow to warm up, so spring comes slowly to the island; but as the days get longer and warmer, the pace begins to quicken. The cool, crisp May days, when the sky seems a particularly brilliant blue and white gulls soar overhead, are truly beautiful. The banging of hammers, the smell of paint—those white houses have to be painted all the time due to the dampness—the launching of boats, and the repairing of lobster pots by fishers in Menemsha are certain harbingers of another season approaching. Shops and restaurants once again clean, paint, and decorate to prepare for summer, which officially begins in mid-June. Actually, most places open on Memorial Day weekend or a bit earlier. As the days go by, houses and cottages are opened and gardens planted. The shipyards accelerate their work schedules to a frenzied pace as they rush to paint, repair, and launch boats, and ferry reservations become harder to obtain without advance planning.

The visitor at this time of year will find the days crisp and cool, so swimming is out, but a picnic on the beach out of the cool wind coming off the water can be very pleasant. An early-spring drive around the island is a joy, as the shadbush is in bloom—one of the first signs of spring—with showery, white flowers cascading from its branches. The chirp of pinkletinks (the local name for spring peepers) can be heard from the ponds; along the roadways and sandy shores, white beach-plum blossoms burst into bloom. With the trees still bare and the beaches still empty, the island's outlines stand out vividly at this time of year, particularly when you view them from the Up-Island hills. From there it looks as though the island has withdrawn a little while longer before being temporarily "loaned out" to visitors for another season.

Whatever the season you choose to come, you'll find this island unique and interesting.

No More Winter Blahs

Not too many years ago the Island was very quiet in winter: Many stores were closed and there was little to do. A new resident called his first winter "Funny February and Mad March" to describe the idiosyncratic behaviour of some of the residents.

Many older residents, however, prefer the solitude. There's always time to linger on Main Street and chat about the latest event in town. One woman who loved the quiet winters was heard to complain to a friend, "Last year it was that *Jaws* movie, and this year it's the new sewers. You can't have any peace. What's the town coming to?"

There's always time to tend to a crisis, but off-season even the tiniest event gets full attention. A pigeon lay wounded on the sidewalk in front of Edgartown's Old Whaling Church. The animal control officer arrived quickly and informed the police chief of his mission. "Did you give it mouth to mouth?" he was asked.

Nowadays, with a winter population of 14,000, increased transportation, two performing arts centers, an excellent skating rink, a swimming pool, as well as sporting events, winters are less "funny and mad." That wonderful, quirky individuality—the Yankee wit—is fast disappearing.

EDGARTOWN
OAK BLUFFS
WHARF

4

How to Get There

You can reach Martha's Vineyard by air, by ferry, or in your own boat. Choosing which form of transportation to take will require some planning; your choice will be determined by how much time you have to spend in getting to the island and whether you will want your own car on the island or prefer to leave your car in New Bedford (and fly or ferry) or in Falmouth (and take a ferry).

Car

The most commonly used transportation to the island are the ferries and cruise boats, which sail from four different towns and are easily reached by car. One ferry port is New Bedford, an hours drive south of Cape Cod on the Massachusetts coast. Two others are Woods Hole, which is at the beginning, or shoulder, of Cape Cod, and Falmouth, adjacent to Woods Hole. Ferries also originate in Hyannis, which is midway along the south shore of the Cape (locally referred to as the mid-Cape area).

To get to the Cape, it might be helpful for you to know the mileage from key cities.

Washington, D.C.—Woods Hole	478 miles
New York—Woods Hole	271 miles
Hartford, Conn.—Woods Hole	187 miles
Providence, R.I.—Woods Hole	85 miles
Boston—Woods Hole	85 miles

It is about 20 miles from the Cape Cod Canal to Hyannis or Falmouth and a bit longer to Woods Hole.

A crowded Oak Bluffs Harbor on a hot summer day.

With the summer traffic it can take you longer to reach the Cape than at other times of the year, so be sure to allow yourself extra driving time. It might take an hour to drive from the Cape Cod Canal to Hyannis in summer traffic.

Driving from New York City to Woods Hole may take six hours. Take I–95 to Providence; from there take I–195 east to Cape Cod. There are numerous signs to the Cape and Islands. At the Bourne Bridge, which spans the Cape Cod Canal, follow the signs to Falmouth and Woods Hole. As you enter Falmouth, you'll see a large Steamship Authority parking lot for those who want to leave their cars on the mainland. There is a shuttle bus service from this parking lot down to the ferry at Woods Hole.

The drive from Boston to Woods Hole takes about two hours in moderate traffic, but it can take much longer in heavy summer traffic. From downtown Boston take the Southeast

Expressway (Route 3), turn right just before the Sagamore Bridge (which also spans the Cape Cod Canal), follow the canal for 3 miles to the Bourne Bridge, and follow the signs to Falmouth. If you're going to Hyannis, take the Sagamore Bridge over the Cape Cod Canal, and continue on the mid-Cape highway (Route 6) to Route 132, which leads down to Hyannis.

If you're planning to leave your car on the mainland, you'll save an hour or more in driving time by taking the New Bedford Ferry, which is for passengers only. Take exit 15 in New Bedford and head south toward the waterfront. Follow the Vineyard Ferry signs to Leonard's Wharf. The parking lot is a distance from the ferry wharf, so allow yourself plenty of time.

Train and Bus

There is Amtrak rail service from New York City to Providence and Boston, where bus service is available to Hyannis and Woods Hole. Bonanza Bus Lines provides frequent bus service from Boston's South Station and Logan Airport to Woods Hole, stopping in Bourne and Falmouth en route.

Bus service is also provided to Hyannis and Woods Hole from the New York City Port Authority Terminal (212–564–8484). Bonanza meets most Woods Hole ferries, providing direct service to South Station and Logan Airport. There are also private limousine services from the Woods Hole and Hyannis Ferry docks to Boston, Logan Airport, or other cities you request.

A new bus service will connect Kingston—the last stop on Boston's South Shore commuter rail—with Woods Hole. Buses will pick up passengers at the station. The one-way fare, which includes bus and ferry ticket, is $12. Tickets may be purchased through the Woods Hole Steamship Authority or the Plymouth and Brockton Street Railway Company. There are thirteen round-trips a day, and cars may park at the Kingston MBTA lot situated near the Independence Mall.

A regular summer activity among children is diving for coins alongside the Oak Bluffs ferry wharf.

Cruise Ship and Ferry

If you leave your car on the mainland when you visit the Vineyard, you have more choices as to which cruise ship to take. There are three places where these ships originate: in New Bedford, which avoids all the Cape Cod congestion and summer traffic; in Woods Hole or Falmouth at the beginning of the Cape (or what is locally known as the upper Cape); or in Hyannis, which is midway along the south shore of the Cape. Hyannis may be a good choice if you are staying on the Cape and visiting the Vineyard.

The New Bedford Ferry lands in Vineyard Haven, the Falmouth and Hyannis Ferries go to Oak Bluffs, and the Woods Hole Ferry (the only one to take cars) runs to Vineyard Haven and Oak Bluffs. One small passenger-only boat goes to Edgartown.

The New Bedford—Martha's Vineyard cruise ship *Schamonchi,* which carries passengers and bicycles only, sails daily from Leonard's Wharf. The cruise across Buzzards Bay and down Vineyard Sound to Vineyard Haven takes one hour and forty-five minutes. The ship has a cocktail and snack bar and makes three trips a day and four on weekends. It operates spring through fall, and no reservations are needed. The one-way fare is $9.50 for adults and $5.50 for children ages five through twelve; for those under five it's free. A bicycle costs $2.50. Call (508) 997–1688 for more information.

From Falmouth Harbor the *Island Queen,* a small, very pleasant cruise ship, sails to Oak Bluffs eight times a day from mid-June to mid-September. Four trips are made from mid-September to mid-October on weekdays. Late boats run on weekends only. The *Island Queen* carries passengers and bicycles only, and snack food is sold on the ship. It is a forty-minute ride. Adult fare one-way is $6.00, or $12.00 round-trip. Children under thirteen are $3.00 one-way and $6.00 round-trip. Bicycles are $3.00 one-way and $6.00 round-trip. Call (508) 548–4800 for more information. The company also has special buses that meet the morning trips for a complete, two-and-one-half-hour narrated tour of the island. The *Pied Piper* from Falmouth Marine to Edgartown—passengers only—makes five trips daily in season. Adults one-way,

Feeding the seagulls that follow the ferries back and forth all summer long.

$12.50; children under twelve, $8.00. Call (508) 548–9400; by reservation only. Bicycles $6.00 round-trip. Parking $10.00 per day.

Hy-Line Cruises operates boats from the Ocean Street dock in Hyannis to Oak Bluffs, making several trips a day from late April through October. They carry passengers and bicycles only and have a snack bar and cocktail lounge. It takes one and a half hours to cruise across the sound to the island. Adult fare one-way is $12.00. The one-way fare for kids ages five through twelve is $6.00, and children four and under ride free. Bicycles are $5.00 one-way. Hy-Line also runs a ferry from Oak Bluffs to Nantucket. Adults pay $12.00 one-way; children five to twelve are $6.00, four and under are free. Call (508) 693–0112 (508) 775–7185 for more information.

The Woods Hole, Martha's Vineyard, and Nantucket Steamship Authority is the only ferry line to the Vineyard that carries cars as well as bicycles and passengers. It also carries the greatest number of passengers. From mid-June to mid-September the ferries make about thirty trips a day from Woods Hole to Vineyard Haven or Oak Bluffs. It is a forty-five minute trip to either port. Car reservations should be made weeks in advance for the busy season. For information and advance automobile reservations, call (508) 477–8600. The telephones get very busy, so if you are on the island, the best thing to do is to go to the reservation office at the Martha's Vineyard Airport. The Authority's mailing address is P.O. Box 284, Woods Hole, MA 02543. Reservations are required Friday through Monday from mid-May through Labor Day. No standby on these summer weekends; this is to avoid the terrible traffic jams in Woods Hole and Vineyard Haven. The auto rate one-way between Woods Hole and the Vineyard from May 15 to October 14 is $47; early spring and late fall, $28; midwinter, $21. Adult passenger fare one-way is $5.00; children age five to twelve one-way is $2.50. Bicycle fare one-way is $3.00. All the Authority boats have snack bars. The Authority now has new penalties for changing or canceling auto reservations. Be sure to check with them.

Sea Comm Transport, a daily commuter ferry for passengers only, runs from Onset Harbor in Wareham, 7 miles west of the Bourne Bridge. It's a convenient commute from Boston and avoids the congestion at the Cape Cod Canal. Parking is free and the fare is $18 one-way, $30 round-trip. There is a forty passenger limit, and the trip takes about one hour and thirty-five minutes. There are two round-trips per day. For reservations call (508) 295–1448.

Bear in mind that all ferries are subject to small price increases and that parking lot fees vary from $7.00 to $10.00 per day, so it is best to inquire.

Private Boat

If you'd like to sail to the island in your own boat, there are four harbors offering dockage facilities. Menemsha, at the western end of the island, has a small, attractive harbor with slips that provide electricity. For details call the harbormaster at (508) 645–2846. Vineyard Haven has moorings, dockage with plug-ins, launch service, and marina services. The harbormaster can be reached at (508) 696–4249. Oak Bluffs has a tightly packed, U-shaped harbor. Motorboat or sailboat slips with plug-ins and marina services (508–693–4355) are available, and there are some moorings out in the harbor. (It is very crowded in mid-summer.) The harbormaster at (508) 627–4746 rents the moorings. Edgartown has no plug-in facilities, which has helped to keep the waterfront from becoming too cluttered. Moorings out in the harbor are available for rent by the day, week, or season. The shipyard provides marina services.

There are now pump-out facilities for boats in Edgartown Harbor. After extensive studies Edgartown has initiated innovative regulations to keep the harbor clean, and they are strictly enforced.

Plane

Air traffic in and out of Martha's Vineyard has increased dramatically in recent years. The airline carriers serving the island constantly vary, but there is always year-round service from the New York area (currently Newark, New Jersey), Boston, New Bedford, Hyannis, Providence, and Nantucket. There may also be seasonal service from Westchester County in New York and Bridgeport or Hartford in Connecticut. It is best to check with your travel agent or the Martha's Vineyard Chamber of Commerce to find out which airlines are currently operating.

Check with your travel agent for airfare from the New York City area. From Boston it is approximately $120 one-way; from Providence, $60. (Parking is $10 in the open.) From New Bedford, Hyannis, and Nantucket, it is approximately $35 one-way, without advance reservations. (All are subject to increases on holiday weekends.)

Taxis meet all regularly scheduled flights at the Martha's Vineyard Airport, and there are several car-rental dealers at the airport.

Private planes have access to the Martha's Vineyard Airport, but in the height of the summer season there may be so much congestion that you should call ahead to make sure there is adequate space for your plane. Call (508) 693–7022. Private planes also land at the small airport in Edgartown, where the landing field is a grass strip.

5

How to Get Around

If you arrive on the Vineyard without your own form of transportation, you will be pleased to find taxis and buses available, as well as car, bicycle, and moped rentals.

Taxi

Taxis meet all the ferries and scheduled plane flights. Taxi fare between any of the Down-Island towns and the Martha's Vineyard Airport is $10. West of the airport, to the towns of West Tisbury, Chilmark, Menemsha, and Aquinnah, the general charge is $30 to $35 per hour for up to four passengers.

Some year-round taxi companies serving the Down-Island towns are:

Marlene's Taxi, Vineyard Haven, 693–0037.
Atlantic Cab, Oak Bluffs, 693–7110.
All Island Taxi, Oak Bluffs, 693–2929 or (800) 540–3705.
Stagecoach Taxi, 627–4566
Patti's Taxi, Vineyard Haven, 693–1663
Jon's Taxi, Edgartown, 627–4677

Bus

There is now islandwide bus service, and the Up-Island schedule from late June through early September includes Chilmark, West Tisbury, Aquinnah, and the airport. Shuttle bus service between the three Down-Island towns runs from mid-May to mid-October. In the summer season the buses run twice an hour, and during the spring and fall they run hourly. The bus stops are next to the ferry ticket office in Vineyard Haven, behind the police station beside Ocean Park in Oak

Bluffs, and on Church Street across from the Old Whaling Church in Edgartown.

Edgartown provides a seasonal bus service from the outside of town into the center of town. You may park your car on the edge of Edgartown in the parking lot behind the post office, which is at the juncture of the inland road to Vineyard Haven and the road to Oak Bluffs. You also may park in the school parking lot just off upper Main Street. Parking is free. The buses run every fifteen minutes to downtown. It is advisable to use this bus system, as parking in Edgartown and traffic congestion become big problems in the summertime. The other Edgartown shuttle service, the open Tivoli Trolley Bus, leaves from Church and Main Streets by the Whaling Church and goes to South Beach every half-hour. The ride costs $1.50.

There are also tour buses in Vineyard Haven and Oak Bluffs that meet the ferries and offer around-the-island tours, as well as service to the airport and Aquinnah. Advance reservations are not necessary. The trip around the island takes about two hours, and those buses that go out to Gay Head Cliffs stay long enough for the passengers to get a quick lunch at one of the food take-out places there. Taxi vans also meet the ferries at Vineyard Haven. Passengers can share the van, if they wish, for a sightseeing tour. The charge is $30 and up, depending on the number of passengers and the length of time for the tour. There is continuous daily shuttle service in Vineyard Haven between the ferries and a town parking lot off the State Road.

Bicycle, Moped, and Car Rental

These rentals are available in the three Down-Island towns. The majority are in Vineyard Haven, clustered near the ferry dock, while those in Oak Bluffs are, for the most part, right at the beginning of Circuit Avenue and the adjacent harbor area. Edgartown has a couple of bicycle-rental places, and no moped rentals.

Listings of all types of vehicles can be found in both the yellow pages of the local phone book and the newspapers. The car rentals include Hertz, Atlantic, Thrifty, Budget, and Sears.

To rent a car during the busiest times in midsummer or on big holiday weekends, it's best to reserve one ahead of time. Ask the hotel or inn for assistance, or check with your local travel agent.

Bicycling

Bicycling on the island is a great deal of fun because the Vineyard has varied terrain. It will be helpful for you to know the distances and terrain if you're thinking about bicycling around the island. Look for the bike paths in many areas.

From Vineyard Haven to:

Oak Bluffs (via shore route), *flat, one hill* . 3.4 miles
Edgartown (via shore route), *flat, one hill* . 9 miles
Edgartown (on the inland road), *hilly* . . . . . 8 miles
West Tisbury, *partly hilly* . . . . 7 miles
Chilmark Center, *hilly* . . . . 12 miles
Aquinnah, *very hilly* . . . . 19 miles
Airport, *partly hilly* . . . . 5 miles

From Oak Bluffs to:

Edgartown (via shore route), *flat* . . . . 5.5 miles
South Beach at Katama, *flat* . . . . 9 miles
Aquinnah, *hilly* . . . . 20 miles
Chilmark (via Airport Road), *partly hilly* . . 16 miles

From Edgartown to:

South Beach at Katama, *flat* . . . . 3 miles
West Tisbury, *hilly* . . . . 8.5 miles
Airport, *hilly* . . . . 4.5 miles
Cape Pogue and Wasque Beach
on Chappy, *one hill* . . . . 3 miles

From West Tisbury to:

Chilmark Center, *hilly* . . . . 5.4 miles
Aquinnah, *very hilly* . . . . 10.5 miles

From Chilmark Center to:

Aquinnah, *very hilly* . . . . 6 miles

Menemsha, *one hill* . . . . 2 miles
Menemsha to North Tisbury
(via the North Road), *hilly* . . . . 6.5 miles

From North Tisbury to:

Vineyard Haven (via the State Road),
one hill . . . . 6.5 miles
The Lambert's Cove Road, a loop off State Road,
hilly . . . . 4.5 miles

Some of This, Some of That. . .

For newcomers, the Island idiom—those colloquial phrases that are generic to Island life—may sound strange. "On-island from off" describes a visitor; "off from on" a resident. A favorite adjective among the old timers is "some;" some good, some bad, some lucky, etc. Up-Island and Down-Island may confuse the newcomer, too. Down-Island describes the towns on the eastern end of the Island: Oak Bluffs, Edgartown, and Vineyard Haven. Up-Island, which is the western end of the Island, includes West Tisbury (which is really in the center of the Island) and North Tisbury, Chilmark, and Gay Head (which changed its name to Aquinnah, the Wampanoag Indian name) at the western tip.

Severe stormy weather always brings familiar queries among the townspeople in the stores, post office, and other gathering spots: "Are the boats running?" or "Did you get stuck on the other side?"

Before World War II everyone seemed to know everyone else in the small villages and gossip was rampant. And as in so many other small towns, gossip always lingered—unlike urban life where it is quickly diffused. Because Main Street was, and still is, a source of news in the Down-Island towns, the expression "the street says" was germane to the latest political event.

If you take time to understand the Island and its people a little bit, you'll find it well-mannered, charming, quirky, and a little different here. And to the Islanders, visitors come in all stripes and behaviour—summer people, summer not.

Sailboats in Vineyard Haven Harbor

There are special bike paths between Oak Bluffs and Edgartown, alongshore between Vineyard Haven and Edgartown on the inland road, alongside the state forest on the Edgartown–West Tisbury Road, Barnes Road from the airport to the inland Vineyard Haven–Edgartown Road near the high school, and from Edgartown out to South Beach. More are being planned, so watch for them. There is also a small ferry to take your bike across Menemsha Harbor to the flat Lobsterville Road. This avoids the steep hills from Chilmark Center to Aquinnah.

Locking up your bicycle while you do errands or go sightseeing in the three Down-Island towns is necessary because of the enormous number of bike riders on the island. The towns now have bike racks; watch for them. Bikes and mopeds aren't allowed in the towns' centers.

6

Where to Stay

Your choice of a place to stay on the Vineyard will depend on the type of holiday you prefer. Every sort of lodging is available, including inns, hotels, motels, rental houses, efficiency apartments, cottages, campgrounds, and a hostel (though you will not find all of these in every town). A complete list of accommodations is available from the Chamber of Commerce; the following list consists of the author's recommendations.

With few exceptions, the inns on the island resemble bed-and-breakfast places in other areas. Some are very elegant, while others are simple. Most provide a continental breakfast, and some serve a full breakfast. A few places with dining rooms that are open for lunch and dinner also serve the general public.

Most of the historic inns are furnished with antiques and have limited outdoor space, so they are not appropriate for small children. The efficiency apartments or larger hotels with separate cottages that have open grounds and a pool or beach are much more relaxing for a family.

Some places are open on a seasonal basis, from early spring to the middle of autumn; others are open year-round. The rates vary according to the seasons. The general rule of thumb is that summer (in season) is from June to mid-September. Spring and fall rates encompass April, May, and mid-September to mid-November. Winter rates at year-round places are the least costly. In-season prices can range from $70 per night for a double room to $300 and up for a suite in the finest places.

If you're planning a week's stay, apartments, cottages, or two-room suites with kitchenettes are convenient and economical. Prices for these efficiency units range from $500 to $2,500 per week, depending on location, size, and number of occupants. Off-season rates are at least 30 percent less; it's best to inquire about them.

Private homes are available through various real estate offices in the towns. Most are listed with the Chamber of Commerce. Rates run from several thousand dollars per month to over $50,000 for the largest waterfront homes for half a season. On-site inspection is always the best idea for any long-term rentals.

If you are planning a summer visit to the island, the earlier you make your reservation the better; January is not too soon. If you wait until spring, you may not be able to obtain your first choice in the hotels or inns, some of which have cottages and suites that are always in demand.

In this guide the general in-season price range per night for two is as follows: expensive, $250 and up; moderate, $150–$250; and inexpensive, up to $150.

Edgartown

There are many inns, hotels, shops, and restaurants within easy walking distance in this town, and three large public beaches within 2 or 3 miles of town. Edgartown is especially popular in the summer months, so be sure to make a reservation as early as possible. The following is a selection of some of the charming places to stay.

Inns

The Point Way Inn
Main Street
(508) 627–8633
Open year-round. Bed and breakfast. Moderate to expensive.

With a change in ownership, the inn has been completely remodeled. The bright, freshly painted rooms all have air-conditioning, and the artists-owners' attractive contemporary sculpture highlights the garden.

Guests can opt to have the continental breakfast, which includes waffles, in the newly redecorated dining room or out on the terrace. Tea and cookies are served in the garden in the afternoon. The inn also provides a complimentary guest car on a shared basis.

The Charlotte Inn
South Summer Street
(508) 627–4751
Open year-round. Expensive.

There are several nineteenth-century houses in this inn complex, which has beautifully landscaped grounds and attractively appointed guest rooms, which lends elegance and charm to the whole compound. The rooms are furnished with French and English antiques. A complimentary continental breakfast is included, and a full breakfast is available. The inn's excellent restaurant, L'etoile, serves lunch and dinner to the general public and has limited hours in the winter.

The Daggett Houses
North Water Street
(508) 627–4600
Open year-round. Moderate to expensive.

The dining room, on the lower level, is the original part of this historic building and opens onto a lawn that stretches down to the waterfront. The owners call it the Chimney Room, because of the unique beehive construction of the fireplace, said to be similar to one built in Plymouth, Massachusetts, in 1667. The room was the first tavern on Martha's Vineyard to sell beer and ale. In 1660 the "taverner," John Daggett, was fined five shillings for "selling strong liquor." In 1750 the Daggett House was added to the building. Centuries-old pine paneling and beams, whale harpoons, and primitive iron Betty lamps and old whale-oil lamps decorate the Chimney Room.

Through the years Daggett House has been a customhouse, a sailor's boardinghouse, a store, and, during the whaling era, a countinghouse.

Across North Water Street another house has been added to the inn, with extremely nice efficiency units, available by the night or weekly.

The Shiverick Inn, a bed-and-breakfast inn in Edgartown, is decorated for the Christmas holidays.

Guests are served a delicious complimentary breakfast, and dinner is available by reservation, Thursday through Saturday May to November. Both are available to the general public by reservation. AAA Three Diamond rated. Beer and wine are available.

The Shiverick Inn
Pease Point Way
(508) 627–3797
Open year-round. Bed and breakfast. Moderate to expensive.

Built in 1840 during the height of the whaling era by the town's leading physician, this is one of Edgartown's most elegant inns. Although it was originally a foursquare Greek Revival house, additions and changes were made through the years, many by the original owner's widow, who was impressed by the grandeur of southern mansions. The large front hall with high ceilings, sweeping staircase, and early maritime paintings is a striking introduction to the taste with which the rooms have been decorated. Through the front hall is a bright, cheerful sunroom, an adjoining breakfast room, and a small terrace. On the second floor there are eleven large rooms with baths and an outside deck for all the guests to use as well as a two-room suite. The attractive rooms are furnished with antiques, canopied beds, and fireplaces. They are also decorated with pretty country wallpapers and have a great deal of charm. A morning newspaper to enjoy with a delicious continental breakfast is included.

The Edgartown Inn
North Water Street
(508) 627–4794
Seasonal. Bed and breakfast. Moderate to expensive.

Profits from a successful whaling voyage around the Horn to the Pacific in 1798 enabled Captain Thomas Worth to build this home. His son, William Jenkins Worth, was successful in a different type of career when he became a hero in the Mexican-American War and gave Fort Worth, Texas, its name. The second owner turned the house into an inn, and it has been one ever since.

Through the years well-known historical figures have stayed at the inn, including Daniel Webster. Nathaniel Hawthorne came for a rest, and he not only became romantically linked with the innkeeper's daughter, but was inspired to write an essay about the Edgartown marble carver, which appeared in *Twice-Told Tales.*

Located close to the center of the village, the inn is decorated with Victorian and other antiques, and there are interesting artifacts everywhere. The door of each of the twelve rooms in the main house has a brass plaque with the name of someone who was part of the inn's long history. A delicious country breakfast is served in the attractive, open courtyard in back as well as in the colorful breakfast room.

Across the courtyard the Garden House has two spacious rooms with balconies, each room furnished with white wicker and decorated with delightful, summery Laura Ashley–type curtains, wallpapers, and bedding. Adjacent to the Garden House is The Barn, which also has colorful rooms that have either private or semiprivate baths.

The Colonial Inn
North Water Street
(508) 726–4711
Open year-round. Moderate to expensive.

"No effort will be spared to promote the comfort and pleasure of all guests," the *Vineyard Gazette* reported in 1911 when this large building in Edgartown's center was completed. Remodeled several times in the intervening years, the first floor is now a complex of shops and the second, third, and fourth floors are guest rooms and suites.

The forty-two rooms are light and airy and of ample size. They are simply decorated with brass beds, a natural wood armoire for the color cable television, private baths, air conditioning, and telephone. On the fourth floor a small porch provides a spectacular view of Edgartown Harbor out to South Beach and over Chappaquiddick Island. The inn serves a continental breakfast, and a full breakfast is available in several restaurants nearby. Its a AAA Three Diamond and Mobil Three Star inn.

The Shiretown Inn
North Water Street
(508) 627–3353
Seasonal. Bed and breakfast. Inexpensive to expensive.

The two adjoining eighteenth-century houses that make up the inn have the small, original rooms typical of this early period and other rooms that have been opened up to provide suites. They are decorated mostly in furniture of the late Victorian period, and all have private baths. Some have their own private entrances.

Behind the small, intimate courtyard in the back is a most attractive dining room and bar in a separate building. A complimentary breakfast is served here for guests, and dinner is available to the general public. Behind the dining area is a row of old carriage houses that have been converted into inexpensive, small, plain motel rooms. There is off-street parking.

Tuscany Inn
22 North Water Street
(508) 627–5999
Open May–December. Expensive.

Lush linens and crisp colors mark the attractive eight rooms in this new inn. Located in the heart of town, the inn also serves a superb full breakfast on the terrace or in the breakfast room. TV on request. No telephones.

Hob Knob Inn
128 Main Street
(508) 627–9510 or (800) 696–2723
Open year-round. Expensive.

This is a charming spot, with sixteen spacious rooms furnished with a mix of antiques and comfortable pieces. A delicious full breakfast is available on the terrace or in the dining room, and afternoon tea is also served. Bicycles are available for rent as well as the inn's 27-foot Boston whaler for fishing and sightseeing. They will also provide a picnic lunch. Children twelve and up are welcome.

148 Main Street
(508) 627–7248
Open year-round. Moderate to expensive.

This completely restored 1840s whaling captain's house has a heated pool and Jacuzzi in the attractively landscaped backyard. The four spacious bedrooms and the suite in the carriage house are bright and cheerful, with unpainted pine furniture, TV, and phones. Children ten and older are welcome, and a rollaway bed is available. The full breakfast is served in the dining room, on the terrace, or in the bedroom. This is a charming addition to Edgartown's hostelries.

Hotels

Harborside Inn
South Water Street
(508) 627–4321
Seasonal. Handicapped access on ground floor. Inexpensive to expensive.

A step off Main Street are three large whaling captains' houses with the names of the original owners over the doorways. Inside and beyond, the buildings have been radically changed and enlarged. With two newer buildings on either side, the Harborside Inn is now a U-shaped, time-sharing, large resort complex around a swimming pool and boat piers that extend out into the harbor. There are eighty-nine rooms and suites. Both motorboats and sailboats are for rent here, and sailing instruction is also available. Adjacent to the complex is the Navigator Restaurant and Boat Bar. Many rooms have balconies looking out on the harbor, and all have TV, air conditioning, and a refrigerator. No meals are included in the room cost. Suitable for children.

The Edgartown Heritage Hotel
Upper Main Street
(508) 627–5161
Open year-round. Handicapped access. Moderate.

This contemporary, thirty-four-room hotel is tastefully decorated in reproduction antiques. The rooms are cheerful and large with modern baths, color television (satellite system), radio, individual telephones, and air conditioning. The hotel serves a continental breakfast, and next door Fernando's Restaurant, which is open for dinner, is very good. There are conference rooms and a hair salon on the premises. The individually climate-controlled rooms make it very comfortable in the off-season. There is ample parking in the rear.

The Harborview Hotel
Starbuck Neck
(508) 627–7000
Open year-round. Handicapped access. Expensive.

This grande dame of Vineyard hotels, whose original 1891 building is now restored, is a beloved island landmark. The 127 bright, cheery rooms, including the modern addition in the rear, have private baths, telephones, air conditioning, and color television. The apartments and white clapboard townhouses in this twelve-acre complex have fully equipped kitchens, and they are ideal for children.

The front veranda of the original building is furnished with period-piece old-fashioned rocking chairs where guests may enjoy a sweeping view across the pond to the handsome Edgartown Lighthouse, which marks the entrance to Edgartown Harbor. Sailboats and yachts move through the outer harbor, and Chappaquiddick Island is in the distance. There are tennis courts, a large heated pool surrounded by lush gardens, a croquet court in the back, and a swimming beach by the lighthouse in the front. This gracious jewel has been an island favorite for more than a century.

The hotel provides baby-sitting, laundry, and valet services. There's a very attractive café and a large, first-rate dining room serving breakfast, lunch, and dinner.

The Kelly House
Kelly Street
(508) 627–7900
Seasonal. Handicapped access. Moderate to expensive.

The main building was an eighteenth-century inn, but there are now several more buildings, which comprise sixty rooms in all, some with kitchen units. While the Colonial decor is charming, such modern conveniences as a television, air conditioning, and a telephone in each room are welcome, and there's a complimentary continental breakfast. A swimming pool and the inn's tennis courts are nearby, and baby-sitting, valet, and laundry services are provided. Located in the center of town, it's adjacent to, but not on, the harbor. The inn's pub, with the original eighteenth-century rough-hewn beams and ballast brick walls, is delightful, as is the light fare served from 11:00 A.M. to 11:00 P.M. daily.

Apartments

Fligor Apartments
North Summer Street
(508) 627–4722
Seasonal. Moderate.

Trim and neat, economical and very quiet, but only two blocks from the center of town, these four attractive housekeeping cottage units are a real find in Edgartown. Bright and cheery, they have contemporary motel furnishings and telephones, TV, air conditioning, and heat. There's also one two-bedroom house.

Edgartown Commons
Pease Point Way
(508) 627–4671
Seasonal. Inexpensive to moderate.

Two blocks from the center of town is a complex of thirty-five efficiency apartments with motel rooms and a playground area with swings, sandbox, and slides. There are a small, fenced-in pool and shuffleboard on the grounds. All the units have kitchens and color television. The largest of the units, simply furnished in a conventional manner, can accommodate six people; it has two bedrooms and a sofa bed in the living room. There is ample parking. Some apartments are in the large, old main building, which was originally the North School. The small lane running between the back of this building and the pool area is Mill Street, once the site of one of the town's gristmills.

Katama Shores Inn
South Beach
(508) 627–4747
Seasonal. Handicapped access on ground floor. Inexpensive to expensive.

Three miles from Edgartown on the Atlantic Ocean is the South Beach, which is called Katama (an Indian name meaning "great fishing place") by most people. It was here that a large Navy barracks was built during World War II. It has become, with remodeling and numerous additions, a hotel complex of sixty-seven units of rooms, suites, and cottages. All rooms have a private bath, television, telephone, and refrigerator, and some have kitchenettes. The largest cottage on the grounds has six rooms, a porch, a fireplace, and a grill; it is available by the week only.

Surrounded by open fields, the inn is just a five-minute walk over the dunes to the ocean beach. Ideal for children, the inn is plain but convenient, and accommodations include tennis, heated swimming pool, shuffleboard, bicycle rentals, and a restaurant open for breakfast, lunch, and dinner.

Oak Bluffs

There are many bed-and-breakfast places in Oak Bluffs, but only one large, old-fashioned hotel and one attractive motel a half-mile from town. Many vacationers live on their powerboats or rent one of the little gingerbread-trimmed houses or the much larger Carpenter Gothic houses.

Lined primarily with powerboats along the U-shaped harbor, the dock's boardwalk is a cluster of gift shops, eight restaurants, and a marine store. It is also the port for the *Island Queen* ferry from Falmouth and the Hyannis Hy-Line boats. (The dock for the large Woods Hole ferries is outside the harbor.)

The larger gingerbread houses in Oak Bluffs along Seaview Avenue.

Island Inn
Beach Road (P.O. Box 1585)
(508) 693–2002
Open year-round. Handicapped access. Inexpensive to moderate

This sprawling motel complex is set in a grove of oak and pine trees overlooking a golf course and Nantucket Sound. Each of the fifty-one units has a kitchen, fireplace, private bath, color television, telephone, and air conditioning, and they are much more tastefully decorated than the average motel room. One new, two-story building in the complex has high ceilings with bleached timbers and post-and-beam construction. Some rooms have a circular staircase to a loft bedroom with bath. The older suites are a bit larger than other rooms. The cabins facing the golf course have their own porches. Convenient for families with children, the complex has tennis courts, a swimming pool, and Lola's, a very good restaurant serving breakfast and dinner.

The Oak House
Seaview and Pequot Avenue (P.O. Box 299)
(508) 693–4187
Open May–October. Bed and breakfast. Inexpensive to moderate.

A few blocks from the center of Oak Bluffs, on the shore road to Edgartown, is this large Victorian home, the summer residence of Massachusetts Governor Claflin in the 1870s. The house has dark-stained oak paneling everywhere and period-piece wicker and Victorian furniture. Guests can enjoy the sunroom and the spacious living room with its piano. The handsome exterior has a large, open veranda enclosed by a magnificently carved railing and pastel-painted, fancy shingles. The ten guest rooms, four with shared baths, are bright and sunny. Many look out on Nantucket Sound, which is just across the road. A continental breakfast and afternoon tea are served. Children over ten are welcome.

Beach House Inn
Seaview Avenue
(508) 693–3955
Open year-round. Inexpensive.

Queen-size brass beds, wicker, a bit of Victorian furniture—nothing fancy—and the beach right across the street make this an inviting, typically Oak Bluffs inn. There's TV in each room, and a complimentary breakfast is served.

The Wesley Hotel
Lake Avenue (P.O. Box 1207)
(508) 693–6611
Seasonal. Bed and breakfast. Handicapped access. Inexpensive to moderate.

Near the center of town, facing Oak Bluffs Harbor, is this four-story, gingerbread-trimmed hotel remaining from the turn of the century, when Oak Bluffs was in its heyday. At that time there were several huge hotels in town, but they were eventually destroyed by fire.

The striking exterior, with its rococo, Carpenter Gothic trim, has a long veranda facing the busy Oak Bluffs Harbor, which is just across the street. The foyer has retained its antique decor, including an old-fashioned registration desk, heavy, dark-stained oak trim, and old photographs on the wall; an attractive cocktail lounge has been added. The first floor has some new bedrooms that are especially convenient for the handicapped. A continental breakfast is served. Children are welcome.

The front rooms look out to the harbor filled with powerboats and the ferries that run back and forth to Cape Cod.

Vineyard Haven

Vineyard Haven, the island's business center, has a few places to stay within easy walking distance of the town. It has many shops and some good restaurants, but because it is a dry town, it is much quieter in the evening than are Oak Bluffs and Edgartown. It has one small town beach near the ferry wharf, extending to Owen Park, and boat, bike, car, moped, and sailboard rentals are easily available along the waterfront. The town has a large residential area heading out toward the West Chop Lighthouse, where there are many house rentals. You may bring your own alcoholic beverages.

Captain Dexter House
100 Main Street (P.O. Box 2457)
(508) 693–6564
Seasonal. Bed and breakfast. Inexpensive.

Captain Rodolphus Dexter's former home, built in 1843, is just as one imagines an exquisitely furnished mid-nineteenth-century home should look. There are oriental rugs, early American oil paintings, antique brasses, and a Hepplewhite dining room table, where a complimentary breakfast is served. Most of the eight rooms have private baths, and some have fireplaces. The inn is a few steps from the center of town, and there is ample parking. Bring your own alcoholic beverages.

The Thorncroft Inn
278 Main Street (P.O. Box 1022)
(508) 693–3333
Open year-round. Moderate to expensive.

In a delightfully quiet, woodland setting a mile from town, this rambling structure and several smaller buildings on the property are well known for their special appointments: large, tastefully decorated rooms with canopied beds; wood-burning fireplaces; central air conditioning; Jacuzzis or hot tubs in some rooms; TV on request; a full complimentary breakfast; and the *Boston Globe* at your door each morning.

Both afternoon tea and dinner are served to guests, and the inn is entirely nonsmoking. Bring your own alcoholic beverages. Their many awards are well deserved.

Ocean Side Inn
P.O. Box 2700
(508) 693–1296
Open May–November. Bed and breakfast. Handicapped access. Inexpensive to moderate.

The view is spectacular from this home overlooking Vineyard Haven Harbor, only half a block from the center of town. Quiet and private, the inn has spacious grounds reaching down to a sandy beach. The bright, cheerful rooms have televisions, air conditioning, and private baths. There is a complimentary continental breakfast in the summer and ample parking space.

Causeway Harborview
Skiff Avenue
(508) 693–1606
Open year-round. Inexpensive.

Families with children will welcome this sprawling, informal, motel-type complex on the edge of town, but within walking distance. The apartments and cottages all have fully equipped kitchen units, private baths, and TVs. An ample-size pool overlooks Vineyard Haven Harbor in the distance, and laundry facilities are available on the property.

Martha's Place
114 Main Street
(508) 693–0253
Open year-round. Bed and breakfast. Limited handicapped access. Expensive.

Just up Main Street beyond the stone bank, this handsome Greek Revival house overlooking Owen Park has recently been restored. The lovely antiques and oil paintings throughout and the attractive colors make it a very inviting and charming addition to the island's bed-and-breakfast establishments. There is a large dining room table for the continental breakfast, several charming terraces, and Jacuzzis in several rooms; others have fireplaces. The rooms are wired for TV on request, and there's air conditioning throughout. The amenities include afternoon tea, beach chairs, bicycles, box lunches on request, terry robes, hair dryers, and morning newspapers.

The 1720 House
130 Main Street
(508) 693–6407
Open year-round. Inexpensive.

This informal farmhouse with low ceilings, a mixture of antique, contemporary, and collectible furnishings, and six small rooms is for the visitor who wants an inexpensive spot close to town with a very casual relaxed ambience. They serve a continental breakfast and afternoon tea. The house also has a small screened porch and terrace.

West Tisbury

This farming community, which cuts across the middle of the island, is about a twenty-minute drive from the Down-Island towns. It has beaches for residents on the north and south shores and is a charming scenic area with several riding stables. It has very few places to stay other than private homes. A car is a necessity here. The town is dry, so bring your own alcoholic beverages.

The Bayberry Inn
Old Courthouse Road
North Tisbury (Box 546, Vineyard Haven)
(508) 693–1984
Open year-round. Bed and breakfast. Moderate.

Tucked away in a meadow just off the State Road in North Tisbury, the inn is the essence of a small, antiques-filled New England bed-and-breakfast spot. The five bedrooms have bright flowered wallpapers and antique furnishings. The paneled dining room, with its fireplace and nineteenth-century ambience, opens onto a charming terrace where a full complimentary breakfast of blueberry waffles, gingerbread pancakes, or other specialties is served. Horses graze in an adjoining field. Afternoon tea is also available. Beaches, tennis, and horseback riding are nearby. Bring your own alcoholic beverages. Nonsmoking.

The Cove House
Off State Road (P.O. Box 25)
(508) 693–9199
Open year-round. Inexpensive.

These seven one-bedroom apartments located on the south side of the island near the center of West Tisbury are convenient places for a family to stay. They are not fancy but are comfortable, and each unit has a living room with sofa bed, kitchen, bedroom, full bath, TV, and porch. Set in a quiet, rural area with lots of grounds around the building, this is a fine place for children. There's also a pond with a dock for guests to use, and beach passes are provided. The apartments are available for a minimum of three days.

Lambert's Cove Inn
Lambert's Cove Road (RFD, Box 422, Vineyard Haven)
(508) 693–2298
Open year-round. Bed and breakfast. Moderate.

A winding drive through a grove of tall pines reminiscent of northern New England leads to one of the island's superior inns, which measures up to one's expectations in every way: ambience, food, and a gracious country setting. The original part of the house was built in 1790 and greatly enlarged in the 1920s with a barn and carriage house. These have been converted into lovely rooms, attractively decorated with bright, colorful wallpapers, country curtains, and antique and wicker furnishings. There are thirteen rooms in all. Many rooms in the outbuildings have their own porches. The large, comfortable living room in the main building is exceptionally charming and opens onto the porch. The spacious lawns and lilac, boxwood, and wisteria perfectly complement the surroundings.

In the summer season a full breakfast is served to the inn guests, and in the off-season a continental breakfast is included or guests may pay for a full breakfast. Guests may order picnic lunches (in insulated containers). The dining room is open to the general public for dinner and Sunday brunch. Bring your own alcoholic beverages. There's one tennis court, and beach passes to the two West Tisbury beaches are provided.

Chilmark

Having your own means of transportation is a must if you stay in Chilmark. Distances are great to the beaches, restaurants, or grocers, and it's a half-hour drive to the Down-Island towns. There are few places to stay other than private homes. The Chilmark Community Center at Beetlebung Corner is the one gathering place. Like West Tisbury, Chilmark is a dry town.

The Captain R. Flanders House
North Road
(508) 645–3123
Open May–Columbus Day. Inexpensive to moderate.

Surrounded by rolling fields framed by magnificent stone walls, a windmill, and a pond down in the valley, this eighteenth-century farmhouse built by whaling captain Richard Flanders is a period-piece delight. There are eight rooms, a wonderful eighteenth-century house nearby (available by the week), and two charming little one-bedroom buildings on the property, one with a fireplace. A continental breakfast is served on the sunporch and children over four are welcome. Nonsmoking inside. Beach passes are provided. It is featured in Martha Stewart's wedding book.

The Inn at Blueberry Hill
North Road
(508) 645–3322 or (800) 356–3322
Open April–November. Moderate to expensive.

Elegant simplicity describes this delightful compound surrounded by rolling fields dotted with ancient apple and oak trees, blueberry bushes, and lush gardens framed by stone walls.

There are twenty-five rooms in the main building and three cottages. There are also a separate exercise room and a lap pool. Croquet, tennis, and horseshoes are available as well. The rooms, decorated by Carolyn Burgess, the co-owner, feature pine and whitewash, bleached cotton duck, and the work of island artisans. For those who truly appreciate the quiet joys of country comfort and surrounding beauty, this is a treasure. A continental breakfast, lunch, and dinner (changed daily) are served, and picnic baskets are available. Room telephone and TV on request. Nonsmoking rooms. BYOB. Children twelve and up are welcome. Dinner by reservation to the public.

Menemsha

Menemsha Inn and Cottages
North Road
(508) 645–2521
Open April–October. Inexpensive to moderate.

A dirt road leads off the highway just above Menemsha to this inn, which has a marvelous view of Vineyard Sound. There are thirteen efficiency cabins on a hillside that stretches down through the meadows and woods to the beach along the north shore. The view of Vineyard Sound from this camp-like setting is striking, and the cabins are bright and colorful with fresh paint, crisp curtains, and scatter rugs. They are fully equipped housekeeping units (with the exception of linens). Maid service is provided for those who stay more than a week. Each cabin has its own screened porch, picnic table, outdoor grill, and outdoor shower. The inn also has suites and rooms in the main building. The inn has its own tennis court, and beach passes are provided. A continental breakfast is served. Bring your own alcoholic beverages.

Beach Plum Inn
North Road
(508) 645–9454
Seasonal. Expensive.

Another dirt road near the Menemsha Inn driveway leads through the woods to this turn-of-the-century house perched on a bluff overlooking Vineyard Sound. In an eight-acre setting of fields and woodlands, with a tennis court, a professional croquet court, and a fine library, it has, for years, been known for its excellent gourmet food. The guest rooms in the main house and four cottages on the grounds (available by the week) have been a relaxing refuge for prominent individuals in government, business, and the arts.

They serve delicious breakfasts and dinners and provide passes to the local beaches. Bring your own alcoholic beverages. Dinners, by reservation only, for the public. The owners prefer no smoking inside. This is one of New England's superior country inns.

Aquinnah

The Outermost Inn
Rural Route 1, Box 271
Lighthouse Road
(508) 645–3511
Seasonal. Expensive.

Located on the high, rolling moors at the western tip of the island, the inn is surrounded by spectacular views of blue sea everywhere: Vineyard Sound, and the great sweep of the Atlantic Ocean along the south shore. The seven rooms with private baths have a rustic charm, with unpainted furniture in the warm colors of natural woods highlighted by white walls. The large dining room with fireplace looks seaward, as does every room.

They serve a full complimentary breakfast. A delicious dinner (open to the public by reservation) is available Thursday through Sunday. Guests can have cocktails on the porch while enjoying those incredible sunsets. Hugh Taylor, the inn's owner, is one of the singing Taylors, along with James and Kate. Hugh is also an accomplished sailor, and guests can sign up for day sails to Cuttyhunk Island on his 50-foot catamaran. His wife, Jeannie, whose great-great-grandfather was born at the lighthouse, devotes all of her time to running this unique hideaway. A car is a necessity except for the short walk to the beach and the concessions at the Gay Head Cliffs. Bring your own alcoholic beverages.

Duck Inn
Off South Road
(508) 645–9018
Open year-round. Inexpensive to moderate.

Rural with breathtaking views overlooking the Atlantic, and extremely casual and cluttered, this small, old seamen's farmhouse is just a step off the main highway going to the cliffs. The bedrooms are small, and the informal living room, dining room, and kitchen are all one large room decorated in Cape Cod, Southwest, Japanese, and Gay Head Duck. The inn serves a full breakfast and provides beach lunches, and clambakes can be catered. The inn has a cat and a pig. Children are welcome ($8.00).

Up-Island Country Inn
Lobsterville Road
(508) 645–2720
Closed November–March. Moderate.

The term *incredible* best describes the perfectly lovely three-room suites in this charming new inn a step off the

South Road. Tastefully furnished, the three suites include large bedrooms, sitting rooms (with sofa beds), and roomy, modern baths (one with a double shower and a Jacuzzi), making it the ultimate in country comfort. A full breakfast is served in the appealing dining room, with wainscoting and soft Williamsburg green walls to offset the attractive furniture. There is a two-day minimum and, on holidays, a three-day minimum.

Campgrounds and Youth Hostel

Martha's Vineyard Family Campground
Edgartown–Vineyard Haven Road
Vineyard Haven
In season, (508) 693–3772; off-season, (617) 784–3615
Open May–October.

This campground, located 1 mile from Vineyard Haven center, is nestled in a grove of oak trees. It accommodates 180 vehicles. The campground allows one motor vehicle, one large tent, or two small tents per site. There are a recreation hall with table tennis, billiards, and other activities, a playground, a ball field, a camp store, bike rentals, and other facilities. No dogs or motorcycles are allowed. Inquire about rates.

Youth Hostel
West Tisbury Road, West Tisbury
(508) 693–2665
Seasonal. Inexpensive.

Two of West Tisbury's leading citizens, the late Daniel and Lillian Manter, gave this building to the town for a youth hostel. It provides dormitory sleeping and cooking facilities for bicyclists and hikers. The maximum length of stay is three days in summer and longer in the fall and spring. Space is at a premium, so it is best to make a reservation. Members pay $12 per night per person; nonmembers pay $15 per night per person.

Where to Eat

There is a wide variety of eating places on the Vineyard to suit all tastes and preferences. You'll find elegant and expensive restaurants as well as simple family restaurants, plus many places to get a take-out snack or lunch for a day on the beach or bicycling around the Island. Many places are open from the spring through the fall; almost all Up-Island places are closed in the winter.

You may find the less expensive places quite crowded during the busiest time of midsummer, so it's advisable to plan ahead if possible. Some of the more expensive places prefer that you make reservations. Proprietors at the expensive restaurants prefer to have their guests appropriately dressed, with the men in jackets and the women in dressy slacks or dresses; this is particularly true in Edgartown, which is more formal than the other towns. Be sure to inquire about payment when making a reservation; some restaurants take only certain credit cards, and others won't accept personal checks.

The general price range for the various places listed in this book is as follows: expensive, $35 or more per main course, depending on what is included; moderate, $20 to $35; and inexpensive, $10 to $20. A moderate-to-expensive range usually means that the lunch is moderate in cost while the dinner might be $25 or more; inexpensive-to-moderate implies the same kind of price variation. These prices will vary a bit, depending on the extras one might order, and all are subject to fluctuations in the market prices for lobster and swordfish. Those places suitable for children are noted. Others are listed under "Family Restaurants and Take-Out."

Shucking scallops for a wonderful dinner.

Edgartown

L'etoile
Charlotte Inn
South Summer Street
(508) 627–5187
Very expensive.

L'etoile, in the Charlotte Inn, is one of the Island's premier restaurants. The pleasant art-gallery setting is enhanced by an indoor terrace and an outdoor garden with an attractive fountain, flowers, and cool green plantings. It is an ideal background for the excellent French nouvelle cuisine, and the dinner is prix fixe. The wines are superb, and everything is beautifully served.

The restaurant serves lunch and dinner daily in season and on weekends in the winter months. Reservations are necessary. Handicapped access is available.

The Coach House
The Harborview Hotel
North Water Street
(508) 627–7000
Moderate to expensive. Open year-round.

The turn-of-the-century Harborview Hotel is a treasure. Its dining room has a sweeping view of Edgartown's outer harbor and lighthouse. Open for breakfast, lunch, and dinner, the restaurant serves delicious savory selections of fine native seafood—swordfish, lobster, sole, and quahog chowder—as well as lamb, duckling, and beef.

The bar in the dining room opens at 11:00 A.M. Their café, The Breezes, is attractive and guests can take their appetizers, salads, and sandwiches, as well as drinks, out to the porch to enjoy the colorful boating activity in the harbor. Handicapped access. Ample parking. Both open year-round.

The Square Rigger
Upper Main Street
(508) 627–9968
Moderate to expensive.

This old house at the fork in the road on Upper Main Street has been a restaurant for years. An Island favorite, it has a tavern ambience with its plain wood tables, captain's chairs, old beams, and a long bar.

Year after year it is known for delicious steak and seafood specialties that are charbroiled on an open hearth; the lobster choices are exceptional. Dinner nightly from 6.00 P.M. Handicapped access. Open year-round. Take-out also available.

O'Brien's
Upper Main Street
(508) 627–5850
Expensive.

For those who love traditional seafood, meat, and poultry, O'Brien's is a fine choice. It is located in an old white clapboard house on Main Street, two blocks from the center of town. There's a charming white latticed terrace for outdoor dining, as well as a cellar pub and cocktail lounge. Everything is a la carte. Dinner is the only meal served, and the restaurant is open from Easter to October and on Christmas. Reservations are suggested. Handicapped access. Ample parking.

Savoir Fare
Post Office Square
(508) 627–9864
Expensive.

This bright little spot, with its metal umbrella tables in a garden setting, gives no clue to the fact that it is also a superb caterer and one of the Island's top restaurants.

They serve full dinners and light a la carte selections and were recommended by *Gourmet* magazine. Beer and wine available. Closed midwinter. Suitable for children on the terrace. Seasonal. Handicapped access.

The Shiretown Restaurant
Shiretown Inn
North Water Street
(508) 627–6655
Expensive.

One of the island's most charming restaurants is in the Shiretown Inn, two blocks from the center of town. Located in a quiet garden setting in the back of the inn and attractively decorated, this is a delightful indoor-outdoor dining spot, and the dinners are fine. Guests can have a predinner cocktail in the pub adjacent to the dining room or out in the garden.

They serve breakfast, lunch, and dinner daily, and have live entertainment on weekends. Reservations are preferred. There is parking in the rear for guests. The restaurant is open from early spring to late fall. Handicapped access.

Navigator Room and Boathouse Bar
Foot of Main Street
(508) 627–4320
Moderate to expensive.

Located right on the harbor, with a great water view, the

Boathouse Bar has more maritime atmosphere than any other restaurant in Edgartown. The old, exposed beams are hung with ships' lights, wooden blocks, harpoons, fishnets, and lobster buoys. There's a lovely large patio for lunch in good weather. Handicapped access is available.

Upstairs, in the Navigator Room, the atmosphere is slightly more formal than in the Boathouse Bar. Lunch and dinner are served in season, and only dinner is served after Labor Day. Both are closed in the winter. Reservations are unnecessary, but both dining rooms are very popular. Suitable for children outside. Seasonal.

Seafood Shanty
Dock Street
(508) 627–8622
Moderate.

As the name indicates, the savory seafood specialties at this waterfront restaurant are very popular. An island landmark for years, it's open for lunch and dinner during the season. The restaurant also has entertainment and serves light fare in the pub upstairs, which is open from 3:00 to 10:00 P.M. Seasonal. Handicapped access. Children's menu.

Chesca's
Colonial Inn
38 North Water Street
(508) 627–1234
Moderate to expensive.

Located at the Colonial Inn in the heart of Edgartown, this popular restaurant is known for its pasta specialties. There's also a large selection of appetizers and salads. There's a pleasant bar at the back, the decor is attractive, and the facility seats about 130 people. Reservations for six or more only. Open April through October for dinner only.

The tavernlike dining room in the Dagget House in Edgartown dates back to the seventeenth century. It is open to the public for breakfast and dinner by reservation.

Lattanzi's
Post Office Square
(508) 627–8854
Expensive.

Lattanzi's comes in two parts: the beautifully furnished, more formal, expensive restaurant with antique reproductive furniture, brass fixtures, a fireplace, lovely furniture, and fresh flowers; and, adjacent to it, Lattanzi's Pizzeria, which is less formal. It's very attractive, with a fireplace and a large brick oven where the savory pizzas are cooked. The pizzas can be eaten inside or out on the porch tables. No reservations are necessary.

In the formal dining room, they serve the familiar pork, lamb, fish, and beef selections, which have all been prepared in the chef's original, creative manner and are a gourmet's delight. Open for dinner year-round: daily from June through September and Wednesday through Sunday from October through May. Reservations preferred. Handicapped access.

La Cucina Ristorante
Tuscany Inn
22 North Water Street
(508) 627–5999
Very expensive.

This new inn in the heart of town has quickly become known for its excellent Italian food. The gourmet menu of chicken, beef, and fish selections are all treated to the chef's original, creative entrees, making this one of the Island's premier restaurants. Closed mid-January to mid-March. In the late fall (November to January) and early spring (March to May), they have cooking-school weekend packages, which have been most successful.

CJ's
Main Street
(508) 627–8446
Moderate.

West Tisbury's loss was Edgartown's gain when CJ's decided to move to Edgartown. Their entrees and other selections are delicious. The menu changes four times a year to take advantage of seasonal specialties. The decor of maroon tablecloths that pick up the color in the wallpaper adds a nice touch. Open for lunch and dinner, 11:00 A.M. to 11:00 P.M. Open year-round.

The Newes from America
Kelly House
Kelly Street
(508) 627–4397
Inexpensive to moderate.

The eighteenth-century, tavernlike character of this Kelly House hotel pub, with its exposed original beams and brick walls, makes it a delightful spot for a light lunch or dinner. Located in the center of town, it's adjacent to, but not on, the harbor. The clam chowder, salads, lobster rolls, and other familiar choices are quite tasty. Open year-round for lunch and dinner daily. Handicapped access. No reservations required.

Oak Bluffs

Lola's
Beach Road
(508) 693–5007
Inexpensive to moderate.

Adjacent to the Island Inn, Lola's has a large dining area and a pub that serves light fare along with lively, rambunctious entertainment. The specialty here is char-grilled southern seafood, and it's very popular. They also serve a breakfast buffet seasonally, and they have a fine children's menu. Full bar, ample parking, handicapped access. Open year-round.

Stand By Cafe
Oak Bluffs Avenue
(508) 696–0220
Moderate.

This one is a winner and very deceiving—a diner serving gourmet meals! They began serving such fine dinners that they had to require reservations, and guests sit either at the counter or at one of several small tables for four. The decor of crisp, clean Williamsburg green walls and chairs with vintage Oak Bluffs photos enhance the ambience of this delightful spot right near the ferry—hence the name. Open for lunch and dinner year-round. Beer and wine served.

Offshore Ale Co.
35 Kennebec Avenue
(508) 693–2626
Inexpensive.

This new restaurant makes its own distinctive beer right on the premises, the vats visible on the balcony. The tavern-like dark wall paneling, booths, and tables are the ideal background for the moderately priced, fine food and the various home brews. Open year-round, 5:00 P.M. to midnight daily.

Farm Neck Cafe
Barnes Road
(508) 693–3560
Moderate.

There are three sunporch dining rooms in this attractive setting overlooking the Farm Neck Golf Course. The moderately priced food is very good and the lunch menu quite large. Beer and wine are available. They serve breakfast and lunch from April to November, and dinner from June through September. Closed Mondays.

Sweet Life Cafe
Circuit Avenue
(508) 696–0200
Moderate.

This newly renovated Victorian house on the upper end of Circuit Avenue has an attractive courtyard for outside dining, a small porch, and a few tables inside. The reputation of the chef's culinary talents spread quickly, and the entrees ($20–$28) of fish, beef, and poultry are delicious. Open April to January for dinner and for Sunday brunch 10:00 A.M. to 2:00 P.M. Closed Mondays. Handicapped access. Reservations preferred. Beer and wine served.

Season's Bar and Grill
Circuit Avenue
(508) 693–7129
Inexpensive.

Adjacent to the popular Atlantic Connection nightclub is this restaurant, with a very nice bar and grill, serving lunch and dinner daily. Open year-round. Handicapped access.

Brasserie 162
162 Circuit Avenue
(508) 696–6336
Moderate to expensive.

As a departure from the regular New England fare, this attractive restaurant has a Sushi and Tapas Bar, as well as Thai and Cuban dinners. Open for dinner Wednesday through Sunday, May through October. Handicapped access. Liquor served.

Cafe Luna
Dockside
(508) 693–8078
Moderate to expensive.

Located on the harbor boardwalk, it has been completely renovated and painted. Formerly a pizza and sandwich shop, Cafe Luna is now an upscale restaurant serving gourmet lunches and dinners. Seasonal. Handicapped access. Liquor served.

David's Island House
Circuit Avenue
(508) 693–4516
Inexpensive to moderate.

The restaurant was established in 1978 by concert pianist David Crohan, and Island House guests are treated to his delightful classical music and popular improvisations nightly during and after dinner. The cocktail lounge/piano bar is open every night. There is the usual selection of seafood and meat dishes, chowders, and David's special bouillabaisse. The restaurant is open for lunch and dinner May through September. Handicapped access. Liquor served.

Vineyard Haven

There are many small indoor and outdoor cafés along Vineyard Haven's Main Street that all have take-out. They vary in their selections of pizzas, sandwiches, subs, and pastries. There is usually a small courtyard of outdoor tables for those places that are take-out only.

The Black Dog Tavern
Beach Street Extension
(508) 693–9223
Moderate to expensive.

Restless children can play on the beach until meals are served in this well-known eatery on the Vineyard Haven Harbor, with its waterfront-tavern ambience. The dinners

The Black Dog Tavern on Vineyard Haven Harbor

they serve put particular emphasis on local fish, and there's a nice array of simple selections for children. Open year-round for breakfast, lunch, and dinner, with dinner served from 5:00 P.M. to 10:00 P.M. Bring your own alcoholic beverages. No reservations.

Le Grenier French Restaurant
Main Street
(508) 693–4906
Expensive.

This is Vineyard Haven's premier restaurant and one of the Island's best. The chef and owner, from Lyon, France, is imaginative and creates both delicate and delicious French food, and some of the unusual selections are not found in other Island restaurants. The room seats ninety, and the pastel linens, candlelit tables, and skylights provide an attractive atmosphere. Dinner and Sunday brunch are the only meals served here. Located upstairs, and open year-round except for a short period during midwinter; reservations are required. You may bring your own alcoholic beverages.

West Tisbury

Lambert's Cove Inn
Lambert's Cove Road
(508) 693–2298
Moderate.

This charming country inn, with an attractive porch looking out on an old apple orchard, has been featured in *Gourmet* magazine. The very fine dinner selections include lamb, beef, veal, and fish. Both the porch and the large sitting room with fireplace are relaxed and comfortable places to gather before going in to dinner. Their superb Sunday brunch, served from 10:30 A.M. to 2:00 P.M., has become an Island tradition, particularly in the off-season. Dinner is served daily in the summer, and on weekends during the rest of the year. Reservations are requested. Bring your own alcoholic beverages.

North Tisbury

The Red Cat
State Road
(508) 693–9599
Moderate to expensive.

The very simple, plain decor in this small, shingled house in the center of North Tisbury belies the fact they serve extraordinarily fine food. The restaurant seats about sixty-five and serves dinner nightly from 5:00 to 9:00 P.M. Reservations preferred. You may bring your own alcoholic beverages. Seasonal. Handicapped access.

Chilmark

The Feast of Chilmark
Beetlebung Corner
(508) 645–3553
Expensive.

Located in the center of Chilmark, this is a favorite dinner spot for Up-Island vacationers. It has a relaxed atmosphere, with spacious seating, contemporary furniture, and art-decorated walls. The local lamb and fish offerings are delicious, the Seafood Marinara being particularly popular.

There is a separate take-out section where homemade pastries and coffee are available in the morning. While it is not open for lunch, the restaurant is available for private parties anytime. Open May to October. Reservations suggested. Bring your own alcoholic beverages. Handicapped access.

Theo's
The Inn at Blueberry Hill
North Road
(508) 645–3322
Expensive.

The charming Inn at Blueberry Hill is in a lovely mid-island pastoral setting.

Charming simplicity with a blue-and-yellow motif, Hitchcock chairs, and a windowed veranda looking out on a pastoral setting defines the dining room in this country inn. The gourmet dinners, changed nightly, include unusual, creative appetizers; produce from the organic garden or nearby farms; and fish, game hen, lamb, and other offerings. Open nightly to the public, April to December, by reservation, from 7:00 to 9:30 P.M.

Menemsha

Homeport
Menemsha
(508) 645–2679
Moderate.

Overlooking Menemsha Creek, which runs from the harbor into Menemsha Pond, this casual eating place has long been known for its excellent fresh seafood. It's an Island institution, and for years people from the Down-Island towns have brought their cocktails to drink out on the stone jetty or Menemsha Beach and then enjoyed a seafood dinner at Homeport. Open on a seasonal basis for dinner only; reservations necessary. Handicapped access is available. Suitable for children.

Beach Plum Inn
Menemsha
(508) 645–9454
Very expensive.

Hidden away in a lovely setting overlooking Vineyard Sound, this Island landmark is one of the best restaurants for dinner. The seating is limited and reservations are required; but the cuisine is so exceptional that it's well worth finding your way here. They have their own vegetable garden, and the menu changes daily. Alcoholic beverages may be brought to the restaurant. Seasonal.

Aquinnah

The Aquinnah Shop
Gay Head Cliffs
(508) 645–9654
Inexpensive to moderate.

This Island institution is a old favorite, and while the name and management has changed, the tradition of good, inexpensive food for lunch and dinner goes on. They emphasize an American cuisine. The establishment was originally founded at the beginning of World War II by Napoleon Bonaparte Madison, the Wampanoag tribal medicine man and whaler. It has both take-out and tables inside and out on the deck, which hangs over the sea. It's crowded at noon, when most tour buses stop. Seasonal, mid-May to mid-October. Open 11:00 A.M. to 9:00 P.M. Handicapped access. Bring your own alcoholic beverages.

Family Restaurants and Take-Out

Edgartown

Main Street Diner
Old Post Office Square
(508) 627–9337
Inexpensive.

The checkerboard floor and walls decorated with old 1920s beer, Pepsi, Coca-Cola, and cigarette ads set the tone for this perky, reasonably priced eatery. Open year-round, except mid-January to mid-March, from 7:00 A.M. to 10:00 P.M. The sandwiches, salads, homemade muffins, bountiful breakfasts, and some special dinners are very tasty. Take-out also. Handicapped access.

Morning Glory Farm
West Tisbury Road
(508) 627–9003
Inexpensive.

About a half mile from the center of Edgartown is another of those wonderful Island institutions. Originally the owners of the farm, Athearns, sold just plants, fruits, and vegetables at their little barn. But they have since expanded a great deal to everyone's delight. They now sell delicious home baked pastries and pies, cheese, milk, eggs, their own beef and pork, and organic fruits and vegetables. The nice shady lawn is particularly inviting to tired bicyclists to rest and enjoy their food and cold drinks. Open Memorial Day to Thanksgiving.

Seasoned To Taste
Winter Street
(508) 627–7800
Inexpensive.

This small café tucked into the back of Nevin Square, with a little courtyard for a few tables, has been chosen as an Island favorite. Soups, salads, and sandwiches to eat there or take out are very good, and it's well worth a visit. Open daily year-round. Handicapped access. Catering is also available.

Edgartown Pizza
At the Triangle
(508) 627–7770
Inexpensive.

On Upper Main Street opposite The Square Rigger Restaurant, this inexpensive pizza spot has easy parking and tables indoors and out on the deck away from the midtown crowds. The pizzas are tasty, as are the sandwiches; and they also serve beer, wine, and cordials. It's a great spot for children. Open year-round for lunch and dinner. Handicapped access.

Fernando's
Upper Main Street
(508) 627–8344
Inexpensive.

This very affordable family restaurant is open for lunch and dinner. They also have several buffet days and a breakfast buffet on Saturday. The cold bar with lobsters, oysters, clams, shrimp, and crab is very popular. There's plenty of parking next to the A&P. Open year-round. Handicapped access.

The Village Rotisserie
Main Street at the Texaco Station
(508) 627–7784
Inexpensive.

This take-out delicatessen is a winner. It is spotlessly clean; has attractive gourmet items lining the shelves; a dairy case full of basics; and the morning papers. The delicious homemade soups, salads, casseroles, muffins, and sandwiches—the turkey, stuffing, and cranberry being the big favorite—are part of a large menu. There are some fine choices for children. Open late during the summer. Parking in the rear. Open year-round. Handicapped access.

Pizzeria
At Lattanzi's
Post Office Square
(508) 627–9084
Inexpensive.

With tables inside and out on the deck, pizzas cooked in brick ovens, and a bright and cheerful decor, this is a great family spot. The pizzas range from those with baby clams, spinach, and other ingredients to the four European cheeses with tomatoes, and they're very tasty. Open year-round from 5:30 to 11:00 P.M. Handicapped access.

Oak Bluffs

Ocean View Restaurant and Cocktail Lounge
Chapman Avenue
(508) 693–2207
Inexpensive to moderate.

This popular family restaurant, open year-round, is located near the harbor. It is paneled and has square wooden tables, and there is a nice tavern room. The food is good, with many island fish selections. Lunch and dinner are served daily, and reservations are required for six or more guests. Handicapped access is available, as are plenty of parking spaces. Children are welcome.

Linda Jean's Restaurant
Circuit Avenue
(508) 693–4093
Inexpensive.

The homemade food at Linda Jean's, a favorite breakfast spot of Island residents, is fine, as are the hamburgers, sandwiches, and desserts that children enjoy. Open from 6:00 A.M. to 8:00 P.M. daily year-round. Bring your own alcoholic beverages.

Papa's Pizza
Circuit Avenue
(508) 693–1400
Inexpensive.

Butcher-block tables with long wooden benches and old photographs of Oak Bluffs decorate this popular pizza parlor, which has a large selection. Submarine sandwiches are also featured, including the popular Steak Sub Bomb. Beer and wine are served. The eatery is open year-round for lunch and dinner. Handicapped access.

Circuit Café
Circuit Avenue
(508) 693–4585
Inexpensive.

One of the Island's best pizzas can be found at this little bistro, next to DaRosa's stationery store. The sandwiches, grinders, and salads are all reasonably priced; the pizza, delicious. Tables for four inside and on the little porch. Take-out also available. Open year-round. Handicapped access.

Vineyard Haven

M. V. Bagel Authority
96 Main Street
(508) 693–4152
Inexpensive.

Bagels have finally come to the Island in full force, and this attractive indoor-outdoor café is located just across from the stone bank on upper Main Street. The bagels are fine, and the place has become very popular for breakfast and lunch, which includes sandwiches and salads. Open year-round. Handicapped access.

New China
State Road
(508) 696–9800
Inexpensive to moderate.

Across from the miniature golf course on State Road is this nice, quiet spot down below the electronics store. They have tables indoors and out and serve fine Chinese food. Open daily year-round at 11:00 A.M. for lunch and dinner. They also make deliveries. A fine place for children.

The Mystic Grill
Tisbury Marketplace
Beach Road
(508) 693–3324
Inexpensive.

Opposite the pier for the New Bedford Ferry, this is a quiet lunch spot when the ferry isn't arriving or departing. They specialize in vegetarian sandwiches and burgers, as well as regular fare, and have a nice, small gazebo for lunch outside and a few tables inside. Closed January and February. Open in summer from 11:00 A.M. to 7:00 P.M. daily.

The Black Dog Bakery Cafe
157 State Road
(508) 696–8190
Moderate.

On the outskirts of town with convenient parking, this bakery is an off-shoot from the original Black Dog Restaurant. Opening at 6:30 A.M., they serve a fine breakfast and lunch Monday through Saturday. Dinner is served Wednesday through Saturday until 9:00 P.M. Bring your own alcoholic beverages. Open year-round.

North Tisbury

Vineyard Food Shop
North Tisbury
(508) 693–1079
Inexpensive.

An Island institution for many years, and known as Humphrey's, it has the best doughnuts, and some of the best pastries, on the Vineyard. Now they also serve cold drinks, sandwiches, and their famous pies. Their Cuban grilled sandwich, made with ham, pork, salami, and cheese, is very popular. Open daily midspring to midfall. There are tables outside under the trees.

Menemsha

The Menemsha Deli
Basin Road
(508) 645–9902
Inexpensive.

Located right near the Menemsha public beach, this deli offers tasty soups, salads, sandwiches, and desserts that can be picked up here to take to the beach or enjoyed on the premises. Bring your own alcoholic beverages. Seasonal.

Chilmark

Primo's Pizza
Chilmark Store
Beetlebung Corner
(508) 645–3655
Inexpensive.

Located in the center of Chilmark, this country store has a take-out section that offers twenty-five delicious pizzas, some sandwiches, and side snacks. They will take orders for those who want to pick up their food on their way to or from the beach. Primo's is a rare find at the western end of the island, where there are few eating places.

There are many art galleries on the Island and one old favorite is the Field Gallery with Tom Maley's famous frolicsome statuary.

8

Telephone Numbers and Addresses

Here are some important telephone numbers and addresses for your basic needs during your island vacation or to answer your questions before you visit the island.

General

For *emergency* only—fire, police, or ambulance, dial 911
Martha's Vineyard Hospital, Linton Lane, Oak Bluffs, 693–0410
Massachusetts SPCA, Vineyard Haven Road, Edgartown, 627–8662
Animal Health Care, Martha's Vineyard Airport, 693–6515
Massachusetts State Police, Temihigan Avenue, Oak Bluffs, 693–0545
Chilmark Police Headquarters, Beetlebung Corner, 645–3310
Edgartown Police Headquarters, Church Street, 627–4343
Aquinnah Police Headquarters, State Road, Chilmark, 645–2313
Oak Bluffs Police Headquarters, Oak Bluffs Avenue (ferry wharf), 696–4240
Vineyard Haven (Tisbury) Police Headquarters, Beach Road parking lot, 693–0474
West Tisbury Police Headquarters, State Road, 693–0020
U.S. Coast Guard, Menemsha Station, 645–2611
Dukes County Court House, Edgartown, 627–3751

Churches

Edgartown

Edgartown United Methodist Church (Old Whaling Church), Main Street, 627–4442

The West Tisbury First Congregational Church

Faith Community Church, Meeting House Way, 693–6755
Federated Church, South Summer Street, 627–4421
St. Andrew's Episcopal Church, North Summer Street, 627–5330
St. Elizabeth's Roman Catholic Church, Main Street, 627–5017

Oak Bluffs

Apostolic House of Prayer, Pequot Avenue, 693–9470
Our Lady Star of the Sea, Circuit Avenue, 693–0342
Seventh Day Adventist, Martha's Vineyard Hospital Chapel
The Tabernacle (interdenominational), Camp Ground, 693–0525
Trinity Episcopal Church, East Chop Drive, 693–3780
Trinity Methodist Church, Camp Ground, 693–0589
Union Chapel (interdenominational), Circuit Avenue, 693–5350
Christian Science Society, New York Avenue, 696–7369

The ivy-covered St. Andrew's Episcopal Church in Edgartown was built in 1899.

Vineyard Haven

Assembly of God, State Road, 696–7576
First Baptist Church, Spring Street, 693–1539
Grace Episcopal Church, Woodlawn Avenue, 693–0332
Jehovah's Witnesses, Pine Tree Road, 693–3932
Martha's Vineyard Hebrew Center, Centre Street, 693–0745
Christ United Methodist Church, Church Street, 693–0476
St. Augustine's Roman Catholic Church, Franklin Street, 693–0103
The Unitarian Universalist Society of Martha's Vineyard, Main Street, 693–8982

West Tisbury

First Congregational Church, West Tisbury Center, 693–2842
United Methodist Church, Lambert's Cove Road, 693–0476

Chilmark

Chilmark United Methodist Church, Menemsha Crossroads, 645–3100

Aquinnah

Community Baptist Church, Aquinnah Center, 693–1539

Conservation Organizations

There are now eight nonprofit conservation organizations on the island. Each emphasizes a different function, but all of them are concerned with protecting and enhancing the natural beauty of the island and have now joined together for a common cause. They are the Martha's Vineyard Garden Club, Sheriff's Meadow Foundation, Trustees of Reservations, Vineyard Conservation Society, Vineyard Open Land Foundation, Felix Neck Wildlife Sanctuary, Nature Conservancy, and Martha's Vineyard Land Bank, which manages the proceeds from a 2 percent tax on all real estate transactions to acquire farms, beaches, and woodlands for the public benefit. All these conservation organizations' offices are at the Mary P. Wakeman Center on Lambert's Cove Road, West Tisbury, with the exception of the following: The Land Bank and Felix Neck Wildlife Sanctuary are in Edgartown; and The Trustees of Reservations is in Vineyard Haven. Anyone wishing to make a contribution, financial or otherwise, should contact these groups.

Information, General

The Martha's Vineyard Chamber of Commerce is helpful in answering general questions about the island. It is located on Beach Road in Vineyard Haven, two blocks from the ferry wharf. The telephone number is (508) 693–0085. If you are writing to them, use the Beach Road address, Vineyard Haven, MA 02568.

The Edgartown Visitors' Center, located across Church Street from the back of the Old Whaling Church, is another valuable resource. You can find public rest rooms and a post office here in addition to important travel information. Shuttle buses from Vineyard Haven and Oak Bluffs terminate here, as do several chartered bus tours.

Information, Historical

The Vineyard Museum, on School Street in Edgartown, is the island's main museum. The staff there are helpful in answering questions about the Vineyard's history, as well as genealogical queries. The museum also publishes an excellent historical quarterly, *The Dukes County Intelligencer,* which is on sale at their offices along with other publications on the history of the Vineyard. Financial contributions are always welcome, should any visitor care to subscribe to the quarterly or give directly to the museum. The telephone number is 627–4441.

Libraries

Chilmark Public Library, Chilmark Center, 645–3360
Edgartown Public Library, North Water Street, 627–4221
Gale Huntington Library, Vineyard Museum, School Street, Edgartown, 627–4441
Aquinnah Public Library, Aquinnah Center, 645–2314
Oak Bluffs Public Library, Circuit Avenue, 693–9433
Vineyard Haven Public Library, Main Street, 696–4211
West Tisbury Public Library, South Road, 693–3366

Museums

Cottage Museum, Campground, Oak Bluffs
The Vineyard Museum, School Street, Edgartown, 627–4441
Old Schoolhouse, 110 Main Street, Vineyard Haven, 693–9317

U.S. Post Offices and Zip Codes

Aquinnah (Chilmark post office and zip code)
Chilmark, Beetlebung Corner, 645–2535, zip 02535
Edgartown, Upper Main Street, 627–7318, zip 02539
Menemsha, 645–3501, zip 02552 (open May 15–September 15)
Oak Bluffs, Park Avenue, 693–1049, zip 02557
Vineyard Haven, Lagoon Pond Road, 693–2818, zip 02568
West Tisbury, State Road, North Tisbury, and West Tisbury, 693–7899, zip 02575

Translation Services

If you are a foreigner and need help with your English, call or visit the Chamber of Commerce on Beach Street in Vineyard Haven, (508) 693–0085.

After the storm along the South Shore

9

Leisure Activities

Antiques Shops

Browsing in antiques shops is a favorite pastime for many island visitors. You will find antiques and collectibles for sale in all the towns, except Aquinnah. The prices and quality vary a great deal, from simple collectibles to country pine furniture, china, early American brasses, turn-of-the-century wicker, and nineteenth-century furniture and reproductions.

Art Galleries

There are many art galleries in the island towns featuring photographs and paintings. Island scenes in watercolors and prints predominate, but the variety is enormous, from the least expensive lighthouse print to works by well-known artists whose work has been featured in art galleries in New York, Boston, and other urban art centers.

Art Instruction

Many art galleries provide instruction for both children and adults. There are also many individuals and groups that offer instruction in handcrafts, photography, and papermaking. It is best to check with the Chamber of Commerce or the individual galleries.

Beaches

The island beaches are very popular with summer and fall visitors. The gently lapping waves all along the north and northeast sound side of the island are ideal for swimming or launching a sailboard. Some of these beaches are pebbly, while others are wide and sandy. The Atlantic Ocean beaches have very fine sand in most places and coarse sand in others. The size of the surf depends on the weather conditions. Many beaches are open to the general public, but a number of town beaches are open to residents and guests only.

At times the ocean surf along the South Shore from Chappaquiddick to Aquinnah can be rough, with a strong undertow that's dangerous. Vacationers are advised to be cautious and talk to the lifeguards if necessary. Ticks, which can cause Lyme disease, are found in the beach grasses, so it's best to stay away from them.

Chappaquiddick

Cape Pogue Wildlife Refuge and Wasque Reservation are two adjoining beaches on Chappaquiddick Island that run along the east side of the island. They are managed by the Trustees of Reservations and are subject to their regulations. To reach the beach, take the Chappy ferry and go directly across the island on the only paved road, which later becomes a dirt road and leads to the Wasque parking lot. The beach is open to all.

Edgartown

The Lighthouse Beach is at the entrance to Edgartown Harbor, by the lighthouse, and is open to all.

The Katama Beach, the public beach at South Beach, is on the south side of Edgartown. There is a shuttle bus to the beach from the center of town. If you drive here, follow Pease Point Way to the beach, which is 3 miles from town. It is an extremely popular, 3-mile-long barrier beach. There are lifeguards and rest rooms with changing areas. Visitors are constantly asked to pick up their own trash and not to trample or drive on the dunes. Katama, in Indian dialect, means "crab fishing place." A few blocks from Edgartown's center there's a fork in the road, and both paths lead to the beach. The left fork has parking at the Katama Farm and concession stands.

The Edgartown–Oak Bluffs State Beach (called Joseph A. Sylvia Beach) is a 2-mile stretch of open beach along the State Road that runs between Oak Bluffs and Edgartown. It is a fine swimming beach, with some areas more pebbly than others, and it is very popular in midsummer. There are lifeguards at the Edgartown end of the beach, but as on many island beaches, there are no food stands, other than an ice cream truck at the Oak Bluffs end, and no toilet facilities. The beach is open to all.

Oak Bluffs

Oak Buffs Town Beach is a calm, shallow beach with fine sand that runs along either side of the ferry wharf in Oak Bluffs. It is open to all.

Vineyard Haven

Owen Park Beach near the ferry dock on the harbor is a small, sandy beach open to all.

Lake Tashmoo is outside of Vineyard Haven on the north shore. To reach it, you can go out Main Street or Franklin Street, heading toward West Chop. Turn left on Daggett Avenue and follow it to Herring Creek Road, a dirt road that goes down to the beach. The beach is sandy, there is usually a fair current at the entrance to Vineyard Sound, and it is open to all.

West Tisbury

Long Point Wildlife Refuge is located along the Atlantic Ocean and Tisbury Great Pond. It is a 580-acre preserve managed by the Trustees of Reservations. They own a half-mile of South Beach, and swimming, surf fishing, and picnicking are permitted here. There is an admission fee of $2.00 per person ages fifteen and over and a charge of $5.00 per vehicle. There is also a limit of fifty-five cars per day. To reach Long Point, take Deep Bottom Road, which is exactly 1 mile west of the entrance to Martha's Vineyard Airport, and follow the signs along this narrow, bumpy dirt road for 3 miles to the refuge. It is open to all.

Lambert's Cove Beach is on the north shore in West Tisbury. Unlike many areas along the shore where the beach is pebbly, here there is fine sand. The beach is for West Tisbury residents and guests only.

Chilmark and Menemsha

Lucy Vincent Beach is on the south shore facing the Atlantic Ocean. There is a lifeguard on duty, but the beach is open to Chilmark residents and guests only.

Squibnocket Beach on the south shore is a sandy, wide, beautiful beach with long, slow rollers coming ashore. It is open to Chilmark residents and guests only.

Menemsha Town Beach is right beside the stone jetty at the entrance to the harbor. It is a slightly pebbly beach open to all, and the water is gentle and calm. No lifeguard or facilities of any kind are available other than rest rooms.

Aquinnah

Aquinnah Beach is that long stretch of ocean beach you can see from the Gay Head Cliffs, and the road running alongside the beach is called Moshup's Trail. It is open to the public and carefully supervised.

Lobsterville Beach is along the north shore of the island. Because it is a Vineyard Sound beach, the waters are gentle, and the beach is pebbly. All along the road opposite the beach, the low, rolling dunes are a protected tern and gull nesting area. A road here also leads over to Menemsha Pond Beach. This is a public beach, without lifeguard or facilities.

There is no swimming or trespassing on the Gay Head Cliffs or the beach, which is a historic landmark. Moshup Trail Beach is open to the public until you reach Philbin Beach, which is open to Aquinnah residents only. Watch for signs.

Bicycling

The island is noted for its varied, undulating terrain. There are, however, a few flat spots for easy pedaling (see

A popular farmer's market is held twice a week all summer in West Tisbury.

Opening day of trout fishing for the children at Island Ponds.

the bicycle mileage chart on pages 42–43). They are the road from Vineyard Haven to Oak Bluffs and on to Edgartown; a short stretch in mid-island by the airport; and State Road between North Tisbury and Vineyard Haven. The fun of riding around has been greatly improved by the addition of bike paths, which are also safer. Biking through the pines alongside the state forest, out of danger from passing cars, is delightful.

Bird Watching

There are many places to go bird watching on the island. Various groups sponsor bird and nature walks. The Wakeman Center (693–7233) and the Felix Neck Wildlife Sanctuary (627–4850) have information about other groups on the island that also sponsor walks throughout the year.

Boat Rentals and Instruction

The following places have small boats or sailboards for rent, and they also offer instruction. Check with the Chamber of Commerce for other rentals.

Edgartown

The Harborside Inn on South Water Street has both outboard motorboats and small sailboats available, and there are several old wooden schooners offering full- or half-day sails and available for private groups. They also provide instruction. Call 627–4321.

Vineyard Haven

There are many boating options in Vineyard Haven, the home port of an extraordinary number of gaff-rigged wooden vessels; some are new, and some are very old. These sailboats take passengers for full- and half-day sails, as well as weekly charters. The Coastwise Packet Co. has the topsail schooner *Shenandoah* and the pilot schooner *Alabama* for weeklong cruises for children, where they participate in sailing the vessels, as well as adult cruises. Gosnold Cruises has a kids' adventure cruise (one hour), as well as adult cruises in Nantucket and Vineyard Sound. The famous wooden-boat builders Gannon & Benjamin have two boats for charter, and there are others, such as *Liberty, Laissez-Faire,* and *Ayuthia.* It's best to check the phone book's listings for further information.

Wind's Up on the Beach Road has sailboards, catamarans, and Sunfish. Instruction is also available. Call 693–4252.

Aquinnah

Hugh Taylor, owner of the Outermost Inn, has a 50-foot catamaran, *Arabella,* which takes visitors over to Cuttyhunk Island for lunch, or out for sunset sails. The boat is docked in Menemsha. For reservations call the Outermost Inn, 645–3511.

Boat Ramps

For those who have a small boat, it's helpful to know where you can launch it. All the launching ramps are in protected bays and lagoons, but these protected waters lead out to sea for those who want to go offshore for sailing or fishing.

Boat ramps can be found at the following locations:

Edgartown

Anthier's Landing into Sengekontacket Pond; or Katama, at the south end of Katama Bay Road, into Katama Bay.

Vineyard Haven

Beach Road, on the Vineyard Haven side of the lagoon drawbridge, into the lagoon; or Lake Street into Lake Tashmoo.

Oak Bluffs

East Chop Drive, along the north side of Oak Bluffs Harbor, into the harbor; or Medeiros Cove, on the west side of Oak Bluffs, into the lagoon.

Aquinnah

At the Aquinnah-Chilmark town line at Hariph's Creek Bridge, into Nashaquitsa Pond; or Lobsterville, across the creek from Menemsha Harbor, into Menemsha Pond.

Canoeing and Rowing

The increasingly popular Oar and Paddle Association (627–4905) sponsors trips along the north shore, instruction, and a regatta. Check the phone book or Chamber of Commerce for kayak rentals.

Children's Activities

There are about twenty-five different camps for children, and it's best to check with the Chamber of Commerce, or watch for newspaper notices for more information. All towns have playgrounds adjacent to schools. Other activities include:

Art, dance, language, and music instruction; check with the Chamber of Commerce
Playground at the Boys and Girls Club in Edgartown
Miniature golf in Vineyard Haven and Oak Bluffs (see page 118)
Sailing instruction at Sail Martha's Vineyard, Vineyard Haven Yacht Club, and Chilmark Community Center
Tennis clinics available in many towns, as well as the Farm Neck Golf Club, Lyn Puro at the high school, the tennis center at the airport, and the Island Inn, including private lessons.

- Junior golf program available at Mink Meadows Golf Club
- Several gymnastics day camps
- Summer basketball program in Oak Bluffs
- Figure-skating lessons; call The Ice Arena (693–5329)
- Red Cross swimming instruction in Vineyard Haven, Oak Bluffs, Edgartown, and West Tisbury; check with the town halls.
- Public skating daily, beginning in late July; call The Ice Arena (693–4438)
- Children's Theatre, a division of Island Theatre Workshop
- Pony rides at Nip and Tuck Farm in West Tisbury; call for hours (693–1449)
- Story hours at all libraries
- Preschool programs in all towns
- Art, crafts, theater, and photography instruction
- Day camps; tennis, baseball, soccer, and ice hockey camps
- Sports day camp, including sailing, swimming, and arts and crafts, at the St. Pierre Camp, Vineyard Haven
- Riding stables
- Merry-go-round in Oak Bluffs
- Nature and birding walks, canoe safaris, and landscape photography
- Tour of the lobster hatchery in Oak Bluffs, weekday mornings and midafternoons
- Strawberry and raspberry picking at the Thimble Farm off Vineyard Haven–Edgartown Road
- Special programs at the Vineyard Museum
- Many fascinating children's programs all summer long at the Felix Neck Wildlife Sanctuary for kindergarteners through tenth-graders
- World of Reptiles, off Vineyard Haven–Edgartown Road in Edgartown

Gus Ben David, director of the Felix Neck Wildlife Sanctuary, talking to his great horned owl, Midnight, one of the collection of birds, snakes, and lizards at his World of Reptiles.

Concerts

There are many concerts and musical programs all summer long at the Tabernacle, the Chilmark Community Center, the Old Whaling Church, and various other locations. It's advisable to check the schedules in the newspaper each week. Arlo Guthrie, Dave Brubeck, André Previn, Harry Connick, Jr., James Taylor, Carly Simon, and many others have performed on the Vineyard in past summers.

Evening Entertainment

In addition to the many plays, concerts, lectures, and films that go on nightly all summer long, there are three particularly popular places: the Atlantic Connection, the Wintertide Coffee House (both open year-round), and the Hot Tin Roof. They feature nationally known entertainers all summer.

There are also popular restaurants that feature piano bars, jazz groups, and other performers: The Seafood Shanty, O'Brien's, and The Wharf in Edgartown; Lola's, David's Island House, and others in Oak Bluffs; and Wintertide in Vineyard Haven. Check the newspapers for announcements.

Fall Foliage

Unlike the wildflowers, which should never be picked, dried grasses can be gathered in the fall without hurting the plants. The salt hay, oats, and other marsh grasses, milkweed pods, cattails, and bittersweet (which grows everywhere and is destructive but pretty) make very attractive arrangements.

Film, Theater, and Dance

There are four movie theaters in the Down-Island towns, which feature the latest films all summer long. In Oak Bluffs there are two seasonal theaters at the busy intersection at the foot of Circuit Avenue; in Vineyard Haven the theater on Main Street and a new theater in Edgartown are open year-round. For information call 627–7469.

At the Vineyard Playhouse, located on Church Street in Vineyard Haven, a professional New York theater group stages plays and musicals in season (693–6450). The Island Theatre is a year-round community theater for amateurs, both adults and children, that produces plays and musicals. The Yard, a professional dance group from New York, has its own attractive theater in a renovated barn at Beetlebung Corner in Chilmark. The performers, choreographers, composers, and directors live and work within the complex throughout the summer season. Call 645–9662 for details on productions.

Fishing

The tricky tides swirling around the island will largely determine an angler's luck. As many as three different tides

The month-long Martha's Vineyard Striped Bass and Bluefish Tournament includes many prizes for boat and onshore fishing.

are said to converge at Edgartown Harbor. High tide at Aquinnah can vary as much as an hour from that inside Menemsha Pond. High tide at Cape Pogue on Chappaquiddick is eight hours different from that at Aquinnah, and the tide difference between Edgartown and Vineyard Haven is thirty minutes. The *Vineyard Gazette* prints a tide chart each week, and the Eldridge *Tide Book* is helpful in determining when to fish where. Some of the best shore-fishing spots on the island are also some of the most popular. Bluefish, bonito, and striped bass are caught along the Chappaquiddick shore at Cape Pogue and Wasque and at Lobsterville Beach in Aquinnah. Some anglers have luck at the stone jetties at State Beach between Oak Bluffs and Edgartown and at the entrance to Menemsha Harbor. Scup is found in the inner and outer harbors everywhere, while the once plentiful flounder, which prefer the sandy shoals, have become scarce. Don't be concerned if you're a novice and bring in what's locally known as a sand shark; they are harmless and quite common. Cod, which are caught in the cool weather during spring and fall, are not ordinarily considered a game fish, but they have become increasingly popular with sport fishers.

Fishing Offshore

Chartering a boat to go trolling offshore for blues, bluefin tuna, shark, and white marlin is very popular. In Edgartown check with Coops, 627–3909, or Larry's Tackle Shop at 627–5088. In Oak Bluffs call the harbormaster, 693–4355; in Vineyard Haven call 696–4249; and in Menemsha check with the harbormaster at 645–2846. Consult the paper for information about other sailboats and motorboats available for short sightseeing trips or longer cruises.

Flight Instruction

Flying lessons are available at Martha's Vineyard Airport. It is best to go and inquire, as the availability of instructors varies from year to year.

Golf

There are two public golf courses on the island, and they are both Down-Island. Farm Neck Golf Club, which overlooks Sengekontacket Pond and the State Beach, is located off County Road in Oak Bluffs. An eighteen-hole championship course, Farm Neck has a driving range, a fully equipped pro shop with rental equipment, and buckets of balls for the driving range. For further information call 693–2504. The Mink Meadows Golf Club is an eighteen-hole course in West Chop just off Franklin Street. Call 693–0600.

On State Road in Vineyard Haven, there's an eighteen-hole miniature golf course (Island Cove Miniature Golf Course, 693–2611) that is tastefully landscaped with waterfalls and

A game of golf is a good way to appreciate the island's beautiful scenery.

planting. Open spring to fall, it provides handicapped access for the first nine holes.

Dockside's Mini Golf in Oak Bluffs is on the second floor, with an indoor and outdoor nine-hole course.

There is a driving range on the Vineyard Haven–Edgartown Road in Vineyard Haven. They have thirty-six stations, and twelve covered tees.

Horseback Riding

Riding has become increasingly popular on the island; many local children have their own horses, and families summering here for a good part of the season sometimes bring horses with them. Martha's Vineyard South Shore Stables in West Tisbury, along the south shore opposite the airport, is quite large. They operate year-round and offer both children's and adults' classes. For further information call 693–3770. Pond View Farm on New Lane in West Tisbury (693–2949), Misty Meadows Horse Farm on the Old County Road (693–1870), Iron Hill Riding Stables (693–0786), Arrowhead Farm in West Tisbury (693–8831), and The Red Pony in West Tisbury (693–3788) also offer trail rides, lessons, and boarding facilities. There are others, so inquire.

Island Tours

The best way to become acquainted with the island is to take walking tours of the three Down-Island towns and a driving tour of the rest of the island, as described in the last four chapters of this book. There also are guided tours in buses and taxi vans that originate at the ferry landings, as well as a walking tour of Edgartown sponsored by the Vineyard Museum. Taxis are also available for private tours.

Lectures

Lectures on the island are too numerous to list individually. All the churches, performing arts centers, and other public gathering places seem to have their share of lectures each summer. Because there are so many summer visitors in the art, academic, television, and business worlds who volunteer their services for one group or another, the lecture choices are quite unusual. It's best to check your newspaper each week for the upcoming events.

Libraries

Each of the six towns has its own public library. They all have children's reading and storytelling programs. Summer visitors may get library cards, even if they're staying only briefly on the island, and the cards are good for one year.

For twenty-seven years, Mike Wallace of 60 Minutes *has contributed his time and talents to raising money for the Nathan Mayhew Seminars, Vineyard Haven Library, Old Sculpin Art Gallery, Felix Neck Wildlife Sanctuary, Possible Dreams Auction, and other organizations.*

Museums

The island has three interesting museums to visit. They are the Vineyard Museum in Edgartown, the Cottage Museum in Oak Bluffs on the Camp Ground, and the Old Schoolhouse Museum with artifacts from the Seamen's Bethel in Vineyard Haven.

The Vineyard Museum

On School and Cooke Streets in Edgartown is the interesting complex of buildings that make up the Vineyard Museum. The twelve rooms of the Thomas Cooke House are furnished with early island artifacts, including costumes, dolls, a large collection of whaling material, and more.

The main building houses the Gale Huntington Library of History and the Francis Foster Museum. The library is the island's major historical library and repository of documents, log books, and charts used by the Royal Navy during the Revolutionary War, genealogical materials, and thousands of old books about the history of Martha's Vineyard. The Francis Foster Museum houses scrimshaw, whaling material, ship models, maritime paintings, products of early local industries, and a display of Nancy Luce's poetry and tombstones for her pet chickens.

There is a boat shed containing a whaleboat, a peddler's wagon, a Button hand-pump fire engine used from 1854 to 1925 (and in the island's Fourth of July parade), a Noman's Land boat, beautifully woven Indian eel pots, and many other items. Also on the society's property is the old Fresnel lens from the early Gay Head Lighthouse.

The museum's buildings are open daily from 10:00 A.M. to 4:30 P.M. Admission charges are as follows: Adults are $5.00, and children under twelve are $3.00. The museum's telephone number is 627–4441.

Cottage Museum

This antiques-filled gingerbread house on the campground at Trinity Park in Oak Bluffs will delight anyone interested in the interiors of these tiny Carpenter Gothic houses. Open Monday through Saturday during the summer.

Old Schoolhouse with Seamen's Bethel Artifacts

Originally Nathan Mayhew's schoolhouse, and the Daughters of the American Revolution Museum, this charming little building now houses an interesting collection of maritime artifacts from the original Seamen's Bethel, which was down on the waterfront. Ship models, paintings, carved walrus tusks, and other artifacts were donated by sailors for whom the Bethel provided fellowship, housing, and religious services when they came ashore. Open daily during the season (693–9317).

Nature Walks

Nature walks have become increasingly popular in recent years. Because of the migratory flight path over the island and the mild climate, the variety and abundance of flora and birds are unusual. All the wildlife sanctuaries are open for hiking through the woods and alongshore; some also allow picnicking and swimming. Different conservation groups sponsor nature walks, and it's best to check the local paper or call Felix Neck (627–4850) or the Vineyard Conservation Society (693–9588) for information. In addition to the nature walks, both organizations have birding, flora and fauna, and coastal and inland educational tours for adults. Several conservation organizations also offer canoe and kayak trips.

If you're here for a short visit and would like to see four very different areas, the wooded Cedar Tree Neck along the north shore, the flat plains of the mid-island state forest, Chappaquiddick's outer rim at the Wasque Preserve, and Lobsterville's Cranberry Lands will show you the island's enormous natural diversity.

Shell Collecting

The desire to pick up a pretty shell on the beach is irresistible to most people. The shells on the island aren't outstanding, but there are some attractive ones, particularly the scallop shells, which are found near the drawbridge in Vineyard Haven, the Oak Bluffs end of the State Beach near the bridge and jetties, around the Edgartown Lighthouse, and on Lobsterville Beach. There are almost no shells on the south shore.

Shellfishing

If you enjoy the island, the best thing you can do for those who live here is not to go shellfishing at all. It is an important part of the local economy for residents, and the inexperienced or careless visitor can damage the clam beds and kill the baby scallops very easily. There is a great effort now under way to increase the growth and development of clams, oysters, lobsters, and scallops. Abuse of shellfish beds is against the law.

Shopping

There are many gift shops, clothing stores, handcraft shops, and art galleries, as well as T-shirt shops and souvenir stores. There are some very attractive shops with hand-knit sweaters, sport clothes, unusual gifts, and antique and locally made gold jewelry. Many shops carry the work of local craftspeople, from furniture, clothes, quilts, and pottery to lovely weathervanes, and all of the shops are busy on rainy days. The Flea Market, open on Wednesday and Saturday from 9:00 A.M. to 5:00 P.M. in Chilmark, has become extremely popular.

Sports Briefs

The following adult sports (in addition to those previously mentioned), take place at various times year-round: dart tournaments; ice skating at the arena; ice boating if weather permits; small-sailboat races in Menemsha Pond; golf tournaments off-season; Wind-surfing races; lacrosse, softball, and soccer games; nature, environmental, bird, and ecology walks year-round, sponsored by Felix Neck and the Vineyard

Conservation Society; and kayaking and canoeing, which have become very popular. Check with the Wakeman Center.

Tennis

All the towns but Aquinnah now have public tennis courts. In Edgartown there are town courts located behind the Edgartown Fire Department on Robinson Road (no telephone) and at the Martha's Vineyard Regional High School on the Edgartown–Vineyard Haven Road. The private courts on the Katama Road are rented out to the public. In Oak Bluffs the courts at the Island Inn are open to the public (693–6574). There are town courts available on Tuckernuck Avenue (no telephone), as well as at Farm Neck, on the County Road (693–9728). There are two town courts in the center of Vineyard Haven on Church Street, and they have a free clinic for children under fifteen. At the grammar school in West Tisbury on Old County Road, there are courts available. Reservations must be made a day in advance, but there is no telephone. The Chilmark Community Center at Beetlebung Corner has tennis for Chilmark residents and summer visitors staying in the town. The Vineyard Tennis Center at the Airport has two very good indoor courts. Call 696-8000 for information.

Tours and Interesting Places to Visit

The island is full of many interesting places to visit, most of which are included in the museum section of this chapter or in the island tours. In addition, you may enjoy knowing about the following:

Vincent House

The Vincent House on Main Street in Edgartown is owned by the Martha's Vineyard Preservation Trust and is open to the public to demonstrate how houses of the seventeenth century were constructed. Its hours during the summer are 10:00 A.M. to noon, Monday through Friday.

Flying Horses Carousel

This Oak Bluffs carousel, one of the oldest in the nation, is a must-see for island visitors. The handsome wooden horses are more than a century old, and the carousel has been listed on the National Register of Historic Places. It is open from 1:00 to 9:00 P.M. daily, from spring through fall.

Chicama Vineyards

On State Road outside of Vineyard Haven are the Chicama Vineyards. Chicama produces several different kinds of wines from a variety of European grapes. It is the first winery ever licensed in Massachusetts, and visitors may tour the vineyard and the winery. Grapevine wreaths, wine, and gift items are offered for sale. Tours are held from 11:00 A.M. to 5:00 P.M., Monday through Saturday.

State Lobster Hatchery

In Vineyard Haven on Shirley Avenue, off County Road, is the state lobster hatchery. Here, in a laboratory with its tanks and marine biology equipment, valuable research and experiments are being done on the living habits of lobsters. The hatchery is nationally known in the scientific community for its accomplishments in expediting the growth process of lobsters, and an attendant is on duty to explain the work being done here. The hatchery is open daily, year-round, and there is no admission charge.

Wildlife Sanctuaries

The island's wildlife areas are open to the public year-round. They are open, natural areas of woods, beach, marsh, and pond. These sanctuaries are primarily for walking in and enjoying nature in its undisturbed state. The untiring efforts

Wild turkeys roam the fields and woodlands Up-Island.

and financial contributions of many people have made these areas available to the public and kept them from being developed, ensuring that future generations will have the opportunity to enjoy a pristine environment. Approximately 20 percent of the island's total landmass is now protected.

There are guided nature and bird walks, often to raise money for a given sanctuary; these are announced in the paper. There is no admission charge to these wildlife sanctuaries, with the exception of Long Point Wildlife Refuge, and no swimming or picnicking is allowed except where noted below. All of the sanctuaries listed below are easily accessible. There are many others, if you are interested; information on them can be obtained at the Vineyard Conservation Society Office at the Wakeman Conservation Center on Lambert's Cove Road, or the Land Bank office on Main Street in Edgartown.

Edgartown

The Felix Neck Wildlife Sanctuary is located off the Edgartown–Vineyard Haven Road. This is a unique, 350-acre wildlife preserve of beach, marsh, open fields, and woodland. It offers the summer visitor a network of 6 miles of marked nature trails with a photography blind and an observation blind to watch waterfowl on Sengekontacket Pond, and they have some astronomy evenings as well. In the barn there are nature displays, a library, a gift shop, and booklets for sale. They also run a very popular summer day camp for kindergarteners through tenth-graders.

Sheriff's Meadow is a sixteen-acre preserve off Planting Field Way. There are foot trails around Sheriff's Meadow Pond through woods and marshland and along a path that affords a lovely view of Eel Pond and Nantucket Sound.

Wasque Reservation is a 200-acre preserve of dune and beach bordering Katama Bay on the southeast corner of Chappaquiddick. Swimming, picnicking, and fishing are permitted.

Cape Pogue Wildlife Refuge includes the northeast shoreline of Chappaquiddick and runs out to the lighthouse from the Dike Bridge.

The Trustees of Reservations offer three tours on Chappaquiddick: a three-hour over-sand safari ride; a two-hour canoe tour on Cape Pogue Pond; and a ninety-minute tour to the Cape Pogue Lighthouse. For information call 627–3599.

Vineyard Haven

West Chop Woods, off Franklin Street, is an eighty-three-acre preserve owned by the Sheriff's Meadow Foundation. There are marked trails but no facilities of any kind here.

North Tisbury

Cedar Tree Neck is a 250-acre preserve on the north shore that is operated by the Sheriff's Meadow Foundation. From State Road in North Tisbury heading toward Vineyard Haven, take Indian Hill Road to the sanctuary down a very steep, narrow dirt road. There are color-coded, marked trails through the woods and along the beach. It is a fine place for nature study and hiking.

Priester's Pond is a delightful, small (three-acre) preserve at the intersection of State and North Roads just beyond the Liberty Oak Tree in North Tisbury. They allow canoeing, fishing, and picnicking.

West Tisbury

Martha's Vineyard State Forest, practically in the center of the island, is a 4,000-acre preserve in West Tisbury and Edgartown. A marked nature trail begins at the headquarters off Airport Road. There are 14 miles of paved bike paths and fire lanes for horseback riding.

Chilmark

Menemsha Hills Reservation is a 200-acre preserve operated by the Trustees of Reservations. It is located off the North Road, midway between Tabor House Road and Menemsha Cross Road, and there is a parking area. There are marked foot trails leading down to the rocky shore, and picnicking and fishing are permitted.

Middle Road Sanctuary, off Middle Road in Chilmark, is owned by the Sheriff's Meadow Foundation. They now have marked trails, and it's a fine spot for nature study.

Waskosims Rock Reservation features a huge split boulder in the middle of this 185-acre reservation of fields, woods, and streams. Horseback riding, picnicking, and biking are allowed. The entrance is on North Road.

Winter Sports

Winter sports on the island can be a great deal of fun. When there's snow on the ground, cross-country skiers hurry out to the beaches to ski. There is an ice-skating rink in Oak Bluffs on the inland road between Edgartown and Vineyard Haven. Skating lessons, hockey games, and public skating are offered. Telephone the ice arena at 693–4438 for more information. Ice skating is enjoyed on ponds whenever the weather is especially cold.

Some Old Favorites

A weekly visit to the Farmer's Market in West Tisbury.

The Saturday Flea Market at Beetlebung Corner in Chilmark.

Time for a leisurely visit to The Vineyard Museum and time to make a contribution.

The Merry-go-round early in the day when it isn't too crowded.

A morning stroll through one of the cemeteries, and a reminder tracings are not allowed.

A visit to Polly Hill Arboretum

Ice skating on the ponds is very popular, although it usually doesn't last too long.

Tisbury Health Club on Main Street in Vineyard Haven has an indoor swimming pool and exercise classes. Call 693–7400. There are many other exercise classes available.

Winter or Summer Reading

Bookstores on the island stock the best hardcover books and popular paperbacks for the beach. The Bunch of Grapes in Vineyard Haven, the island's premier bookstore, is very large and exceptionally well stocked. The popular Book Den East in Oak Bluffs has a barn full of wonderful used and rare books. In the center of Edgartown, the Bickerton and Ripley Bookstore has a fine selection for rainy-day browsing. The Fligors of Edgartown, a large gift and toy store, has carried books about the island and volumes by island authors for years. They also have a splendid array of children's books. Also check the charming gift shop The Secret Garden, in Oak Bluffs, which has a fine book selection.

There are many nationally and internationally known writers summering or living most of the year on the Vineyard, and the stores give autograph parties for their latest work. It's best to check the newspaper notices for them. Because of the large number of authors, Bickerton and Ripley and Bunch of Grapes have weekly book-signing parties.

Edgartown's Fourth of July Parade

10

Annual Special Events

April

Osprey Festival at Felix Neck, celebrating the return of the ospreys (late March or early April)
Easter-morning sunrise service at the Gay Head Cliffs

May

Windsurfing Races at State Beach (late May)
Spring Plant Sale, Felix Neck Wildlife Sanctuary (late May)
Memorial Day Parade
Memorial Day weekend 5K Road Race

June

Tour of the inns in Oak Bluffs (early June)
Oak Bluffs Harbor Festival (second week of June)
A Taste of the Vineyard, Edgartown (mid-June)
Martha's Vineyard Catch and Release Fly Rod Tournament (late June)

July

East Chop House Tour (early July)
Edgartown's Seafood Festival (first week of July)
Fourth of July parade and fireworks in Edgartown
Oak Bluffs annual house tour (early July)
Tisbury Street Fair (second week of July)
Edgartown Regatta (mid-July)
Portuguese Festival, Oak Bluffs (mid-July)

For twenty years, auctioneer Art Buchwald's wit and expertise at working the crowd has been responsible for the island's most successful fundraiser for Community Services. People bid on such things as a sail with Walter Cronkite, tennis with Mike Wallace, or a few songs from Carly Simon (above).

Shark-fishing tournament, Oak Bluffs (late July)
Vineyard Antiques Show, Edgartown (late July)
Annual Catboat Clambake, Edgartown (late July)
Chilmark dance group "The Yard" annual benefit (late July)

August

Edgartown House Tour (early August)
Edgartown Library's annual antiques show (first week of August)
All Island Art Show, Oak Bluffs (first week of August)

"In the Spirit" festival, Oak Bluffs (first week of August)
Possible Dreams Auction, Edgartown (first week of August)
Camp Meeting Association's Cottage Tour at the Camp Grounds (early August)
Vineyard Museum, Art, Antiques, and Collectibles Annual Auction (second week of August)
Big Game Fishing Tournament, Oak Bluffs (mid-August)
Chilmark Road Race (mid-August)
Boston Ballet, High School (mid-August)
Museum's square dance and barbecue, Chilmark Community Center (mid-August)
Illumination Night, Oak Bluffs (mid-August)
Martha's Vineyard Agricultural Society Fair and Livestock Show, West Tisbury (mid-August)
Martha's Vineyard Pro/Am Tennis Tournament, Oak Bluffs (late August)
Oak Bluffs fireworks (late August)
Kayak Regatta, Sengekontacket Pond (late August)
Boston Pops at the Tabernacle, Oak Bluffs (late August)

September

Vineyard Artisans Festival, West Tisbury (Labor Day weekend)
Tivoli Day Street Fair, Oak Bluffs (second week of September)
Annual Pro-Am Bike Races, Oak Bluffs (second week of September)
"Shine A Light" dinner, Vineyard Museum (mid-September)
Vineyard Haven Harborfest (mid-September)
Martha's Vineyard Annual Striped Bass and Bluefish Derby (mid-September to mid-October)
Vineyard Trade Show, West Tisbury (last week of September)
Windsurfer Challenge, Oak Bluffs State Beach (mid-September)

October

Columbus Day 5K Road Race, Oak Bluffs
Vineyard Craftsmen Art and Craft Fair, Edgartown Elementary School (Columbus Day weekend)

Sharing a treat at the Agricultural Society's annual fair.

Autumn Harvest Dinner Dance, Agricultural Hall (Columbus Day weekend)
Halloween Happy Haunting Events, Edgartown

November

Martha's Vineyard Skating Club Open Competition (mid-November)
Vineyard Artisans Holiday Festival, Agricultural Hall, West Tisbury (Thanksgiving weekend)
Thanksgiving Day 5K Road Race

December

Tisbury's Twelve Days of Christmas (December 1–12)
Edgartown's Old-Fashioned Christmas Celebration (second weekend in December)
Daniel Fisher House Tea and Christmas Open House
First Night Celebration, Vineyard Haven

The "Colossil Fossil," one of the large shingle-style houses built at the turn of the century in East Chop.

11

Island Architecture

The history of Martha's Vineyard is reflected in its houses, both the interiors and the exteriors. There are seven different styles spanning three centuries. The periods overlap, just as they did on the mainland, but with the islanders' natural reluctance to change, the time spans were often longer and exact dates somewhat obscure. None of the original settlers' houses remain, but the earliest houses were Cape style and were built without the benefit of an architect. Most of them have been extensively remodeled, but the Vincent House in Edgartown has not. It is a prime example of an early Cape, and, fortunately, it is open to the public.

There are full, half, and three-quarter Capes. The full Cape has a large central chimney supporting several fireplaces and a symmetrical window placement, with two windows on either side of the front door. The windows have small, square panes, usually twelve-over-twelve. Based on a style from Devon and Cornwall in England, the one-story Cape, held down against the wind by its snug gable roof (whose eaves come down to touch the front door and windows), hugs the ground and generally faces south. The steep shed roof serves as both roof and wall, the ceilings are low, and the tiny, narrow stairs are just inside the entryway, set against the chimney.

There are half Capes with the front door at one end of the house, two windows, and the chimney usually directly above the front door. The three-quarter Cape is also asymmetrical, with two windows on one side of the front door, one window on the other, and an off-center chimney.

The attic room in the Cape was used for sleeping as well as for storing onions, cranberries, smoked herring, and other food that could hang from rafters. A small cellar, often called a root cellar, served as a refrigerator. It was usually a round, brick enclosure resembling a large well, where vegetables, apples, beer, milk, and other foods were kept cold.

The Vincent House in Edgartown, built in the seventeenth century, is a prime example of an early Cape.

There are very few saltbox houses on the Vineyard. This one is in West Tisbury.

As time went on and more materials became available, two-and-a-half-story Capes were built. By the first quarter of the nineteenth century, most of these houses had added a kitchen ell across the rear of the house, which was called a porch by islanders. This addition was very common throughout the Massachusetts Bay Colony. Often a small room in the ell was used for a creamery. With this ell—or lean-to—across the rear of the house, it had a saltbox profile. This design became very common in New England, but there are almost no true saltboxes on the island.

Houses built in the elegant brick Georgian style (1720–1780) do not exist on the island. The wealth came later, during the whaling era. Instead, in this period the Vineyard produced foursquare Colonial houses with modest adaptations of the Georgian style. They were often built by ships' carpenters with the help of books from England. Two separated chimneys provide a central hall plan with a wide staircase, closets by the chimneys, moldings, a paneled fireplace wall, and a kitchen ell with another chimney to accommodate an iron cookstove. The paneled front door has a row of windows at the top to let in light. On the eve of the Revolution, rectangular and elliptical fanlights over the door became popular, as did sidelights, and they were often made of colored glass. Cranberry glass was the most popular; it allowed the light in, while the owner could peek out without being seen. The squared-off pillars on either side of the door are set flat against the building, and the double-hung sash windows have twelve-over-twelve windowpanes.

The brief, post-Revolutionary Federal period (1776–1840) was a time of great prosperity and burgeoning architecture on the island. The newborn nation's carpenters and shipwrights, with the help of architects in many cases, adopted the warm, delicate detail of the Federal style, which architectural historians have called one of America's "greatest architectural achievements." These large, square, five-bay houses show a mastery of composition, restraint, and grace of detail in the

The Captain's House in Edgartown is a good example of Federal and Greek Revival architecture (right).

Greek Revival architecture was popular on the island in the mid-nineteenth century.

The Menemsha boathouse is part of the history of island architecture.

A typical Victorian house in Oak Bluffs.

The Pink Valentine in Oak Bluffs was built during the Victorian period.

balusters around the hip roof. They usually have elliptical arched fanlights and sidelights, a small projecting portico, spiral staircases, and beautifully carved mantels and moldings. Even the fences, enclosing yards of clipped boxwood and yew (instead of sprawling lilacs and roses), are masterpieces of craftwork. Modest adornments from the Federal period are found on Edgartown houses built at this time. Many island houses are transitional, with up-and-coming Greek Revival pillars adorning the portico and the delicately carved roof rails, such as those on the Daniel Fisher House.

By 1840 Greek Revival architecture had swept up the coast from Jefferson's Virginia. This style was best suited to public buildings; however, the classical doorways with pillars and the cool aestheticism of the style appealed to New Englanders, and they adopted it. Edgartown's Methodist Church is the island's outstanding example. To imitate the white limestone of Greek temples, these buildings were painted white, and the tradition has carried on for all the houses.

As the initial fervor for these Greek adaptations subsided, a new era in architecture, named for Queen Victoria, began to appear. The Victorian era was known for its prudishness; this exterior pretense, as evidenced by lace, frills, and skirts on furniture, also found its way into the charming lacy architecture of the period with the invention of the jigsaw and fretsaw, used for scrollwork.

It was an era that the American poet Amy Lowell called "that long set of sentimental hypocrisies known in England as Victoria"; nonetheless, it did produce the fascinating architecture that can be seen in Oak Bluffs. Tents in the Camp Ground were hastily converted into little wooden houses, each with four rooms (a living room and bedroom downstairs and two bedrooms upstairs; the cooking was done in cook tents, and there was no plumbing. All had front porches facing the Tabernacle in the center of the lawn. The lacy, wedding-cake patterns of Carpenter Gothic, with shingles like pigeon feathers, decorated every "wooden tent" on the Camp Ground, making it a landmark in gingerbread architecture. A few other Victorian buildings can be found in the other towns.

The late nineteenth century and early twentieth century saw the birth of the large, popular, shingle-style houses in East Chop and West Chop. Many of these "cottages" were on the bluffs overlooking the sea.

The other structures that have a unique place in the history of island architecture are the fishermen's boathouses. Without them the town of Menemsha, which relates so strongly to the sea, would lose its character and its visual history. These simple, practical workshops are made from white-cedar shingles weathered a silvery gray in the salt air. The lobster pots piled high outside, and the rope blocks, lobster buoys, carpentry tools, potbellied stoves, and all manner of gear cluttering the interior, are the link between the fisherman and his vessel tied up alongside Dutcher's Dock. The fishermen's gray-weathered homes up above the bluff and the fishing fleet give the coastal village its unique character.

12

Vineyard Haven Tour

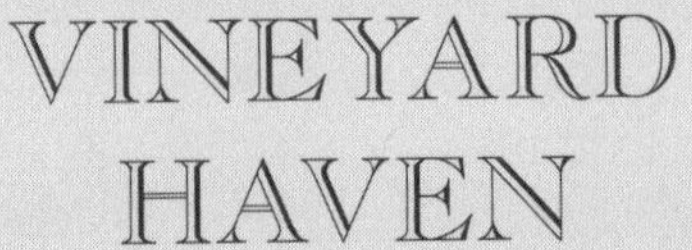

VINEYARD HAVEN

Points of Interest

1. OWEN PARK and OLD SCHOOLHOUSE
2. WILLIAM STREET
3. ASSOCIATION HALL
4. CAPTAIN RICHARD C. LUCE HOUSE
5. JIRAH LUCE HOUSE
6. CHAMBER OF COMMERCE
7. WEST CHOP
8. EAST CHOP

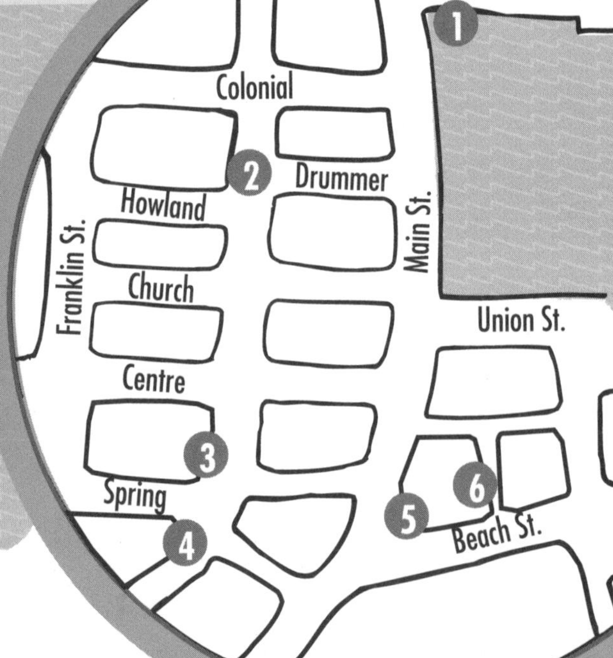

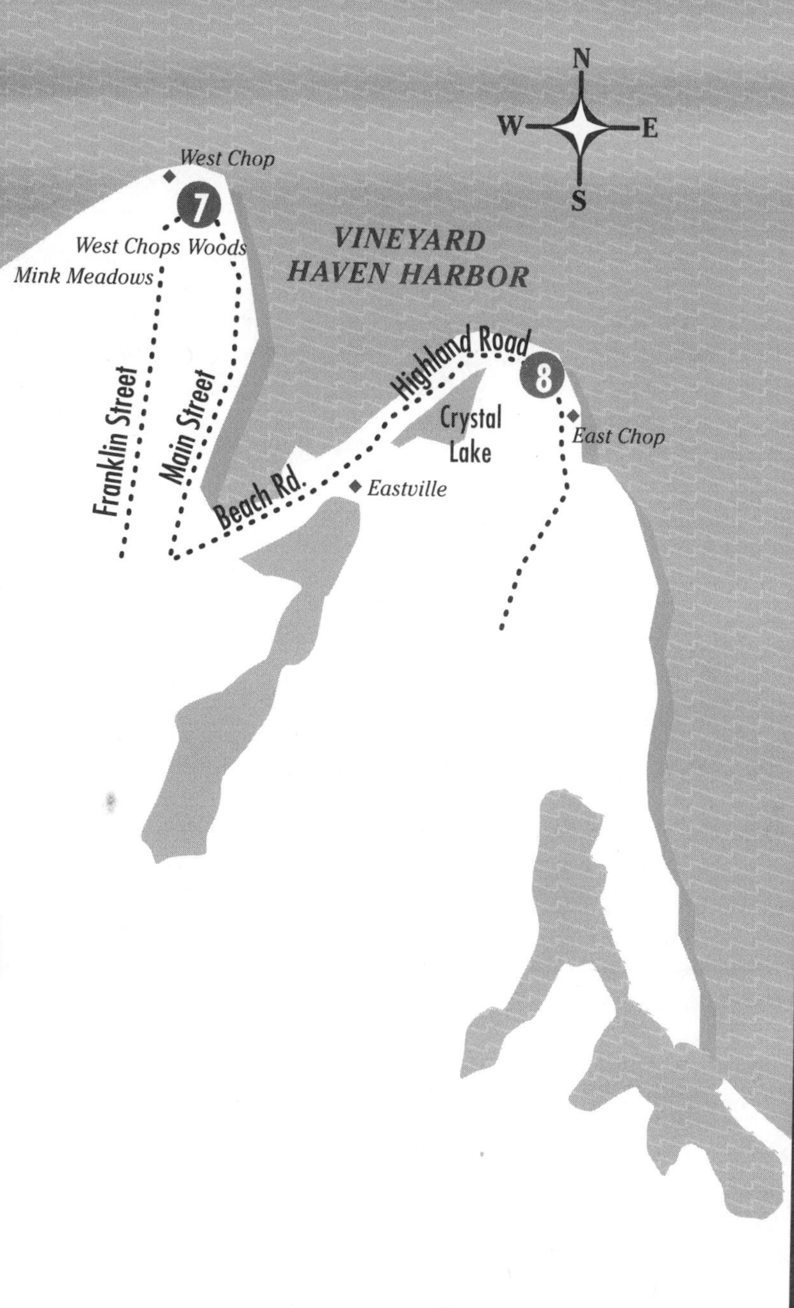
N
W
E
S
West Chop
7
West Chops Woods
Mink Meadows
VINEYARD
HAVEN HARBOR
Franklin Street
Main Street
Highland Road
8
Crystal
Lake
East Chop
Beach Rd.
Eastville

Because Vineyard Haven is the island's commercial center and principal port of entry, we'll begin our first tour here and encircle the island in a clockwise direction.

The first white settlement here began in 1674, thirty-two years after Edgartown, and was known as Holmes Hole for two centuries. In Colonial times it was customary to call a protected anchorage a "hole," while the surname attached to it was usually that of the first person to use it or the owner of the adjoining land.

Holmes Hole was a village within the township of Tisbury. In 1671, when Tisbury received its charter, it was a farming community, and the center of town was the present Up-Island village of West Tisbury. As the little port of Holmes Hole began to grow with the movement of maritime traffic through Vineyard Sound, it separated from West Tisbury, established its own post office, and changed its name to Vineyard Haven in 1871. The town later was legally named Tisbury, however, which is confusing to the newcomer, who will see both names used, although Vineyard Haven is more common.

The growth of Vineyard Haven as an important seaport along the East Coast began with the expansion of trade with the West Indies and coastal shipping. It became a refuge for coastwise traffic, and in the nineteenth century as many as 200 vessels at a time would be in the harbor to replenish supplies, ride out a storm, or wait for a favoring tide and wind. Shipyards, sail lofts, coopers, bakers, blacksmiths, and general stores sprang up along the waterfront to provision the coastal schooners, deepwater vessels, sloops, packets, colliers, and tugs that put into the harbor. Even the men and women who were farmers profited when their "bumboats," which were floating peddler's carts, went out to meet the incoming vessels to sell everything from butter and fresh vegetables to hand-knitted socks.

Neither war nor fire has spared Vineyard Haven in its 300 years. During the American Revolution, when the British Commonwealth could no longer send troops for the island's defense, Vineyarders maintained an uneasy neutrality. In 1778, however, Major General Gray sailed into the harbor with a large force of British troops and eighty-three vessels to replenish supplies. He called together the town authorities, explained his mission, and threatened to burn the town if they resisted. For five days the Vineyard militia was ordered to bring in 300 cattle and thousands of sheep, turn over their arms, and give up public money that belonged to the King of England.

During the War of 1812, Vineyarders were again harassed by the British. Yankee ingenuity was sorely tested in the effort to get supplies through by outwitting and outsailing the British.

On August 11, 1883, tragedy struck the port when a fire, which started in Crocker's Harness Shop (the present site of the Martha's Vineyard National Bank), swept through the center of town and burned sixty buildings on both sides of Main Street. Fifteen years later, in November 1898, a devastating northeaster hit the coast, and fifty vessels in Vineyard Haven Harbor were either driven ashore or sunk at their moorings in what became known as the Portland Gale.

With the opening of the Cape Cod Canal in 1914 and the increased movement of freight along the coast by trains, trucks, and steamships, Vineyard Haven lost most of its maritime commerce. Shipping was slowly replaced by the resort business and the fishing industry; today the harbor is crowded with pleasure boats of every description as well as a small fishing fleet.

The following walking tour is a pleasant way to see the town.

1. Owen Park and Old Schoolhouse Main Street

From the ferry walk up Union Street to Main Street and turn right. A half-block along on the right is the old stone bank, once Crocker's Harness Shop, where the great fire of 1883 started. Continue up the hill, and at the crest the road to your right leads down past the William Barry Owen Park

The Old Mayhew Schoolhouse in Vineyard Haven, which is the Island's seafaring center, contains the Seamen's Bethel Artifacts.

to the small public beach. There are benches, swings, and a bandstand in the park. Given to the town by Mrs. Owen in memory of her husband, whose father was one of Vineyard Haven's foremost whaling captains, it is the only public beach close to the center of town.

Diagonally across the street from the entrance to Owen Park is Nathan Mayhew's old schoolhouse, which has a long history. For many years it was the Daughters of the American Revolution Museum, and it now houses artifacts from the original Seamen's Bethel, which used to be down on the waterfront. For more than a century, the Bethel was a refuge for visiting seamen, and many of the paintings, carved ivory, and ship models were donated by them. Summer hours are 11:00 A.M. to 3:00 P.M. (693–9317).

2. William Street

Return toward town, and just a few steps along, on your right, is Colonial Lane. Proceed up Colonial Lane one block to William Street, the town's handsomest street, which was spared during the great fire of 1883. It is a street of Greek Revival houses, many built by sea captains or others who had profited from the port's prosperity. These formal homes incorporated the latest improvements, such as high ceilings, a parlor heater, a cast-iron kitchen range, and a built-in sink and water pump. The exteriors, embellished with sidelights, fluted columns, and fan-shaped windows, reflected this affluence.

Bear right off Colonial at the corner of William Street for one block to the street's end, where you'll see the gray-shingled Grace Episcopal Church. Turn back down William Street. The houses at this end of the street were built a little later than those at the lower end; some have early Victorian details. As you continue down William Street, you will see at the corner of Church Street the large, fieldstone Methodist Church that was built in 1922 after an earlier one burned. As you approach Spring Street, you'll see the First Baptist Church on your right.

3. Association Hall
Spring Street

Turn right on Spring Street; the second building on your right is the Tisbury Town Hall, also called Association Hall. It was built in 1844 as a Congregational Meetinghouse and was shared by the Baptists at the time. On the second floor is the

Katherine Cornell Memorial Theatre, where many plays, concerts, and community activities take place year-round. The theater has handsome murals depicting the island's history; these were done by Stan Murphy, a local artist. Funds to remodel the theater, as well as to restore the grounds and building, were donated by actress Katherine Cornell, who spent a great part of her life on the island.

4. Captain Richard C. Luce House William Street

Return to William Street. On your right, tucked away in the middle of the block, is a large yellow house, built in 1833. It is the most elegant of the William Street homes. Captain Luce made eighteen whaling voyages before he retired, and it was his home that prompted the building of handsome and stately houses along William Street by sea captains who bought property in the area. Return to Main Street.

A typical nineteenth-century house on historic William Street in Vineyard Haven.

5. *Jirah Luce House*

Bear right on Main Street; at the corner bear left, down toward the water. A few steps on your left is the Jirah Luce House, now a gift shop.

Built in 1804 by Jirah Luce, this is one of the few early buildings to escape the great fire that swept through the center of town. Notice the handsome doorway of this Federal house, made famous by its second owner, Rufus Spaulding. Spaulding was a typical Yankee jack-of-all-trades: physician, postmaster, justice of the peace, innkeeper, and officeholder.

6. *Chamber of Commerce*

Next to the Jirah Luce House is the Chamber of Commerce, where all your questions about the Island can be easily answered. This house is a typical, eighteenth-century building (note the low ceilings) that also managed to escape the great fire.

7. *West Chop*

If you wish to tour the west side of Vineyard Haven Harbor, go back to Main Street and turn right. Head up Main Street past Owen Park to the West Chop Lighthouse, which is 2 miles from town.

The twin headlands of West Chop and East Chop, which cradle Vineyard Haven Harbor, protect this large anchorage from all but a northeast storm. Chop is an Old English term that describes the entrance of a harbor or channel; in the eighteenth century the harbor entrance was called "the neck." West Chop was the site of the first Methodist camp meeting on the Vineyard, in 1827.

While the architecture of the various island communities gives them their visual character, when they began to develop as summer colonies in the late nineteenth century, newcomers had a pronounced influence on their social development. West Chop got its start as a summer colony in 1887, when many reserved Bostonians chose this area. It has, through the years, attracted retired military personnel, educators, and businesspeople, as well as well-known actors, journalists, television personalities, and writers. All the island towns produced renowned mariners, and members of the Eldridge family, who once ran a ferry to Woods Hole and still publish the indispensable *Tide Book,* have long been associated with the West Chop area.

As you drive along the bluff, the houses are a mixture of very old buildings (some moved from other parts of the island), large, turn-of-the-century shingled houses, and some contemporary houses. The road loops around at the West Chop Lighthouse, first built in 1817, and circles around by the West Chop Tennis Club. A right turn here, onto Franklin Street, leads back to Vineyard Haven. After you make this turn, you'll pass the Mink Meadows Public Golf Course and the West Chop Woods, a wildlife sanctuary.

At the end of Franklin Street, bear left to return to the center of Vineyard Haven.

8. East Chop

Back in the center of town, at the five corners by the post office, take the Beach Road for Oak Bluffs. You will see a large

A weekly band concert at the William Barry Owen Park overlooking Vineyard Haven Harbor.

shipyard and Lagoon Pond on your right. With sufficient warning of a northeaster, many boats go into the Lagoon Pond to wait out the gale, just as they did a century or more ago. The lagoon is a good scalloping area, and in the winter months fishing crews can be seen raking the beds from their scallop boats. Also on your right, just before the bridge, is a ramp for launching small boats.

Just over the bridge is a peninsula of land jutting into Vineyard Haven Harbor that is a public beach and a good area for shell collecting. The small cluster of cottages along the waterfront is called Eastville, and the Martha's Vineyard Hospital is on your right. The original settlement here consisted of a ship's chandler, a one-room school, and several taverns. It was also reputed to be the place where mooncussers plied their trade, and it was known locally as the Barbary Coast. By hanging ships' lanterns on poles and swaying them back and forth to resemble a vessel at anchor, mooncussers lured sailing ships onto the rocks, where their wreckage was fair game for looters.

Keeping to the left and staying alongshore, bear left at the next corner onto Highland Drive. It takes you by Crystal Lake, on your right. The lake was known as Ice House Pond in the days before refrigeration, as ice was once cut and stored here. The land around the lake is now a wildlife sanctuary, but it is apt to be too marshy for easy walking.

From the top of the East Chop bluff at the lighthouse, the view across the sound to Cape Cod is spectacular. The lighthouse marks the eastern entrance to Vineyard Haven Harbor and was built in 1877 to replace an 1802 signal tower that had burned.

East Chop was called "The Highlands" in the nineteenth century, when Baptists started their summer camp meetings here. With Methodists living in what is now the center of Oak Bluffs, going by Oak Bluffs Harbor was jokingly referred to as "going over Jordan" (one side Baptist, the other Methodist). The architecture in East Chop is a mixture of Carpenter Gothic and the large turn-of-the-century shingle style. Continue around a sharp curve at the bottom of the bluff; the East Chop Beach Club and Oak Bluffs Harbor are on your left.

Turn left at the end onto Lake Avenue, which leads to the traffic circle at Oak Bluffs.

13

Oak Bluffs Tour

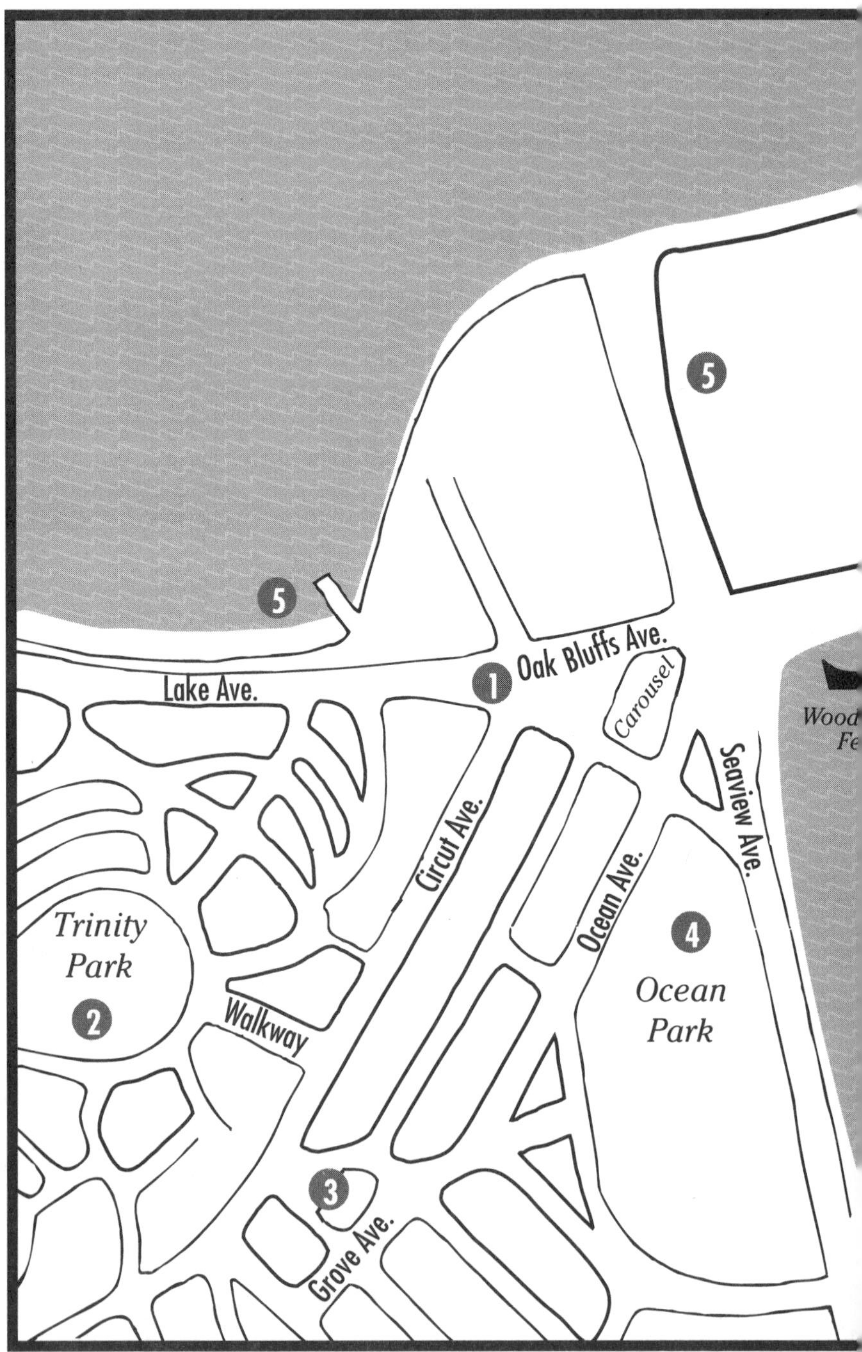
5
5
1
Oak Bluffs Ave.
Lake Ave.
Carousel
Seaview Ave.
Circut Ave.
Ocean Ave.
Trinity
Park
2
Walkway
4
Ocean
Park
3
Grove Ave.

OAK BLUFFS

Points of Interest

1. THE FLYING HORSES
2. TRINITY PARK
3. UNION CHAPEL
4. OCEAN PARK
5. BEACH AND HARBOR
6. ALONGSHORE TO EDGARTOWN

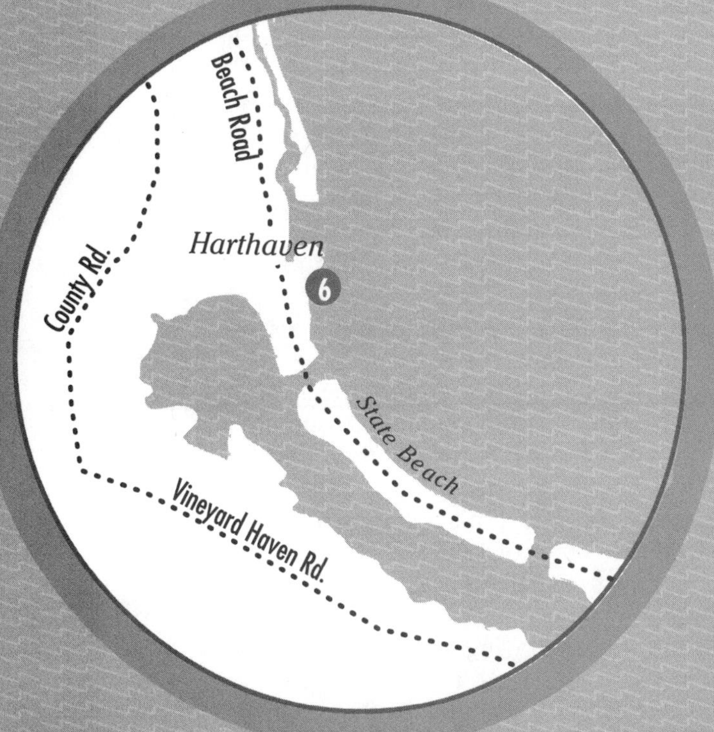

Founded in England in the 1770s by John Wesley, Methodism soon came to America through missionaries; its first appearance on Martha's Vineyard was in 1787, with the arrival of John Saunders, an ex-slave from Virginia. The movement quickly caught fire in America, and in 1827 the first Methodist camp meeting on the island was held in West Chop by "Reformation" John Adams, an itinerant preacher from New Hampshire. The Revivalist service was a public forum for soul searching and emotional displays of doubt and conviction. It was a radical departure from the formality of Congregational services and attracted rich and poor alike. It wasn't until 1835 that the second meeting was held in Wesleyan Grove in Oak Bluffs. Revivalism began to sweep the island, and preachers approached their task with extraordinary zeal as they gathered converts away from the Congregationalists. Their fervor swelled the ranks of those who came to worship in the grove of oak trees.

As the Methodist movement soared, the visitors started pitching their tents in a circle around the speaker's podium. There were family tents and communal tents with partitions down the middle to separate the sexes. In the 1870s a circus-style tent was erected in the center of the Camp Ground for the meetings. This was replaced in 1879 by the present Tabernacle in the center of Trinity Park.

Camp meetings usually lasted about two weeks, but because many members found this seaside "watering spot" delightful, they began staying longer, and in 1864 the first of the "wooden tents" appeared. These tiny cottages, built on the tent sites, were as close together as the original tents, many

A typical Oak Bluffs cottage.

not 2 feet apart. The building boom reached a feverish pitch in the 1870s, when each person tried to outdo the neighbors with Carpenter Gothic decor. The facades were gaily festooned with gables, turrets, spires, scrollwork under the eaves, tiny balconies, rococo verandas, high-pitched roofs, leaded cathedral windows, and intricately cut shingles. The owners painted their lacy valentines in vivid rainbow hues of purple, pink, sea green, blue, and yellow, making this Hansel-and-Gretel village a landmark in gingerbread architecture.

Meanwhile, more and more steamboats were advertising the delights of an island holiday, and the town grew rapidly as a resort for secular visitors, who built cottages, shops, and hotels in the Circuit Avenue and Ocean Park area. Carpenters could scarcely keep up with the booming demands. Hordes of Methodists and vacationers poured off the boats, including cyclists in their club colors; families with trunks, bags, and croquet sets; and young men in straw hats and women in hoop skirts and bonnets.

It was a new era, and working-class people were now taking summer vacations, which were formerly the province of the wealthy. Unlike the aristocratic Edgartown and the commercial Vineyard Haven, Oak Bluffs was a resort and a Methodist meeting place for people from all walks of life. Huge wooden hotels, dance halls (where the song "Tivoli Girl" became a great favorite), a boardwalk, and a roller-skating rink sprang up. It became so lively that the Methodists, wishing to spare their flock the temptations brought by sinful secular visitors, built a 7-foot-high fence all around the Camp Ground. Evidently it wasn't high enough; the holiday spirit prevailed, so they lowered the fence. Not only did the two groups mingle, but one visitor was shocked to hear the strains of "Nearer My God to Thee" wafting out from the roller-skating rink. Croquet games in the Camp Ground reached such a feverish pitch that cheating by ministers' daughters was reported in the local paper.

To celebrate the closing of the religious meetings for the year, the Methodists held Illumination Night near the end of August. The origin of this tradition is obscure. During camp meetings each tent was required to keep a lantern lit at night, which, an observer explained, resembled "the celestial city's pearly gates whose translucence would manifest the beauty of the glorious light within." But it was land developers from outside the Camp Ground who first sponsored a gala Illumination in the summer of 1869 that really lit the place up. The tradition grew until Japanese lanterns hung from every tree, rail, and beam, flickering in a fairyland setting of tiny houses. A Japanese family who had opened a gift shop in Oak Bluffs in the 1870s influenced the decorative character of this annual event, which has continued now for more than a century.

The decline of Oak Bluffs was almost as rapid as its escalation. The hurried overbuilding—in many instances, underfinanced—the financial panic of 1873, and the burning of hotels (suspected to be arson) in the 1890s all contributed to the town's economic demise. But the Camp Ground, while not attracting the hordes it had in the past, continued to attract the Methodists each summer in the little houses surrounding the Tabernacle. The houses have continued to be carefully maintained, sometimes by families of the original owners who have passed them down from generation to generation. They are filled to capacity during the summer. The center of town, which is filled with restaurants, shops, many B&Bs, a few inns, movie theaters, and the Flying Horses carousel, continues to attract many vacationers, and it has grown rapidly in recent years.

You must leave your car near the traffic circle, as the only way to see this fascinating and unique town is on foot. Even bicycles are not permitted in the Camp Ground.

1. The Flying Horses
Circuit Avenue

We'll begin our walking tour at the traffic circle at the foot of Circuit Avenue, which is Oak Bluffs' main street. The Flying Horses is one of the nation's oldest carousels. The handsome wooden horses were carved in 1876 by C. W. F. Dare in New York City and were brought by steamer to Oak Bluffs in 1884. The carousel is a great rainy-day favorite for children. Also, concessionaires in the old building sell souvenirs and cotton candy. The carousel has been listed on the National Register of Historic Places and belongs to the Martha's Vineyard Preservation Trust.

2. Trinity Park
The Camp Grounds
Circuit Avenue

Take the town's main street, Circuit Avenue, which begins across from the carousel. Just before the Secret Garden, on your right, you'll see a sign and the main entrance into the

Camp Ground. Immediately in front of you, in the center of the green, is the large Tabernacle, encircled by a sidewalk and tiny houses. It was erected in 1879 to replace the original meeting tent. Constructed of T-irons, angle irons, pipe, and wooden rafters supporting a corrugated roof, it is one of the largest wrought-iron structures in the United States. Like many sections of the Camp Ground, the Tabernacle is listed on the National Register of Historic Places. Bear right here and circle the Camp Ground in a counterclockwise direction.

The Trinity Methodist Church, the only other building inside the large grassy circle, was built in 1878. Its outstanding feature is the stained-glass cathedral windows. Walk around this fairy-tale setting of gingerbread houses in rainbow colors, each with its wedding-cake trim. Notice one with heart-shaped cutouts, others with scrollwork, cathedral windows, and little spires. They are painted lavender and white, green and orange, yellow and purple, blue and white, and any other combination that highlights the myriad forms of gingerbread. As you stroll around the circle, take time to walk a few steps down the lanes that radiate from the green; they are filled with these tiny "wooden tents."

Return to Circuit Avenue the same way you entered.

3. Union Chapel
Circuit Avenue

Turn right on Circuit Avenue for a few steps, and go directly across the street to the Union Chapel. Built in 1871 during the heyday of the Oak Bluffs land boom, it was for those secular souls who lived outside the Camp Ground's 7-foot fence. "When complete with the spire reaching an altitude of 96 feet," the paper reported, "it will overtop everything." This nondenominational, octagonal chapel with a domed ceiling has a balcony around five sides and eight triangular windows emerging from the rooflike spired dormers. The chapel's consecration was the highlight of a series of festive events that year: the completion of the island's first (and only) drawbridge over the lagoon and the arrival of a new paddle-wheel steamer. The Vineyard Haven band played a new composition especially written to commemorate Tisbury's independence

The Oak Bluffs fireworks are held in mid-August.

from West Tisbury, called "The Bartholomew Gosnold Quickstep!"

4. Ocean Park

Behind the Union Chapel go left on Grove Avenue to Ocean Avenue and continue along to Ocean Park. Stay on this side of the park, which is fringed with large, yet dainty, gingerbread cottages. A band holds evening concerts in the charming gazebo in the center of the park.

As you continue toward the waterfront, the Episcopal Church is on your left, at the intersection of several roads. A Civil War monument is on the right. This statue of a Confederate soldier, painted in lifelike colors and looking like a toy soldier, was commissioned by a Southerner who had moved to the island. It is reputed to be the only such monument erected right after the war by a member of the Confederacy. The plaque reads, THE CHASM IS CLOSED, and it is dedicated to THE UNION VETERANS OF THE CIVIL WAR AND PATRIOTIC CITIZENS OF MARTHA'S VINEYARD IN HONOR OF CONFEDERATE SOLDIERS.

5. Beach and Harbor

Continue past the monument to the waterfront, where the Oak Bluffs Public Beach runs along both sides of the steamship wharf. The area here and back toward the Flying Horses and the traffic circle was once the site of a huge hotel, a roller-skating rink, a dance hall called The Tivoli ("I lov it" spelled backward), and the terminus for the island's only train, the Active, which ran from Oak Bluffs to South Beach via Edgartown for a number of years. When the hotel burned down along with the Active's turnstile, the train continued to run—forward to Edgartown and backward to Oak Bluffs!

Continue along the waterfront toward Oak Bluffs Harbor. You'll pass the public beach and stone jetty marking the entrance to Oak Bluffs Harbor and the pier where ferries from the Cape are docked. A short distance ahead the street terminates at the traffic circle by the Flying Horses, where the walking tour began.

6. Alongshore to Edgartown

Leaving Oak Bluffs for Edgartown along Seaview Avenue, there's a small settlement of houses and an artificially created harbor on the outskirts of Oak Bluffs. Called Harthaven, it is named for the family that originally settled here, and many of the cottages are still owned by members of the Hart family.

Just beyond Harthaven is the beginning of the Joseph A. Sylvia Beach, also called State Beach, which is one of the best swimming beaches on the island. The large body of inland water on your right is Sengekontacket Pond, a favorite spot for bird watchers and a popular scalloping area for Vineyard fishermen in the winter months.

As you continue past the beach and enter the outskirts of Edgartown, there is a fork in the road where the inland road back to Vineyard Haven branches off.

There is a convenient parking lot here, plus bus service to the center of Edgartown and out to the ocean at South Beach. There is another public parking lot at the Edgartown Grammar School. You will want to park your car before touring Edgartown.

The famous Old Whaling Church decorated for Christmas. It is now the Island's performing arts center.

14

Edgartown Tour

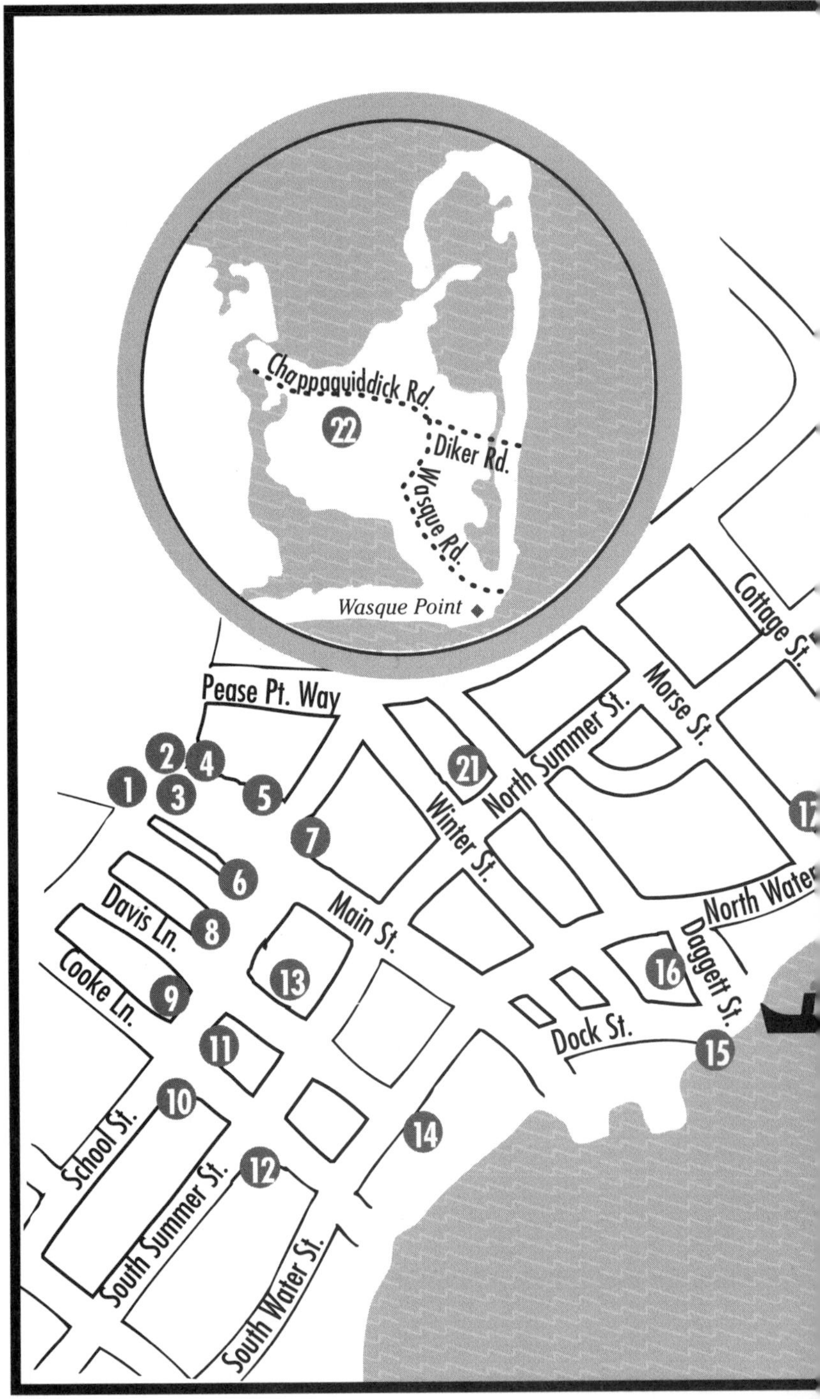
Chappaquiddick Rd.
22
Diker Rd.
Wasque Rd.
Wasque Point
Pease Pt. Way
1
2
3
4
5
6
7
8
9
10
11
12
13
14
15
16
17
21
Davis Ln.
Cooke Ln.
School St.
South Summer St.
South Water St.
Main St.
Winter St.
North Summer St.
Morse St.
Cottage St.
North Water
Daggett St.
Dock St.

EDGARTOWN

Points of Interest

1. START OF TOUR
2. CAPTAIN THOMAS MELLEN HOUSE
3. DR. DANIEL FISHER HOUSE
4. THE VINCENT HOUSE
5. THE OLD WHALING CHURCH
6. ST. ELIZABETH'S CHURCH
7. DUKES COUNTY COURT HOUSE
8. FORMER MASONIC HALL
9. THAXTER ACADEMY
10. THE VINEYARD MUSEUM
11. INTERSECTION OF COOKE AND SCHOOL STREETS
12. FIRST FEDERATED CHURCH
13. THE *VINEYARD GAZETTE* OFFICE
14. PAGODA TREE
15. TOWN DOCK AND CHAPPAQUIDDICK FERRY
16. OLD SCULPIN ART GALLERY
17. THE JOHN O. MORSE GALLERY
18. THE CAPTAIN'S HOUSE
19. THE LIGHTHOUSE
20. EMILY POST HOUSE
21. ST. ANDREW'S EPISCOPAL CHURCH
22. CHAPPAQUIDDICK ISLAND

The first white settlement on Martha's Vineyard was located in Edgartown in 1642. Called Great Harbor by the early settlers, it was a self-sufficient little farming and fishing community. Lacking in trade goods and isolated from maritime traffic moving through Vineyard Sound, the village grew very slowly; it had only thirty-six houses in 1694. But with the gradual increase in island exports and the growth of offshore whaling, the port grew in importance until it reached its peak of prosperity in the nineteenth century.

Just before the American Revolution, Nantucket and Martha's Vineyard owned about one-quarter of America's whaling fleet. Many vessels were commandeered or sunk by the British during the war, and Edgartown's fleet suffered heavy losses. There was a thirty-year hiatus in the local whaling industry, but eventually the fleet was rebuilt, and from about 1820 to the Civil War—a time when many of Edgartown's handsome houses were built—whaling was in its prime. From Greenland to South America, from the Indian Ocean, around the Horn, to the Pacific and Bering Sea, Edgartown's ships sailed on three- and four-year voyages in pursuit of the mammals whose oil and whalebone (the latter used for women's corsets) meant instant riches.

Edgartown provisioned its own fleet and, for a time, that of Nantucket when the large, deep-draft ships needed for long voyages could not get over the sand bar at the entrance to Nantucket Harbor. Nantucket had once been the whaling capital of the world (a title later bestowed on New Bedford); Edgartown's fleet was smaller but prospered well. The wharves along the waterfront were piled high with barrels of oil where whaleships were tied up to unload or to fit out for another long voyage. A bakery turned out hardtack, one of the staples aboard ship. Sail lofts, cooperages, cordwainers, weavers, hat makers, and a tannery were crowded together on Dock Street, along with the glowing forges of smithies. The tangy salt air was tinged with the smells of hot metal, sperm oil, rigging tar, and hemp. Young and old were lured to the waterfront, where they hung around listening to tales of extraordinary voyages, jobs, and prospects of wealth.

When the whaling era ended, Edgartown continued to have a very active fishing fleet. The town got its start as a summer resort when a hotel was built at Katama in 1872. This venture didn't last; but just as Bostonians discovered West Chop, New Yorkers found Edgartown and its handsome houses very charming. Some, following Emily Post's lead, brought strict social mores, and for generations they influenced the reserved character of the community. New Yorkers were joined in Edgartown by people from New Jersey and Philadelphia. Changes came slowly to Edgartown until the 1980s, when many new inns, restaurants, snack shops, and gift shops were introduced in the downtown area. Fortunately, two or three blocks from the center in any direction, you will find attractive houses that keep the town from losing its original character, and it is surprisingly quiet, in spite of the traffic.

Edgartown has narrow streets, and the large houses are built close together, which was common in many New England seaports where the town was built around a harbor. The best way to see the town is a walking tour, and a stroll through the town, day or night, is a delight. It is a tradition in many New England villages to name the houses after the original owner or, in some cases, a famous occupant. You will find many houses on this tour referred to in that manner. There are other fine houses not mentioned, but if you are aware of various architectural periods, you can date the houses yourself as you stroll along.

One additional helpful note: Across Church Street from the back of the Old Whaling Church is the Edgartown Visitors' Center. In addition to providing valuable information, the center houses a post office and public rest rooms. Shuttle buses from Vineyard Haven and Oak Bluffs terminate here, as do several chartered bus tours.

1. Start of Tour

We will begin the tour at the intersection of Upper Main Street and Pease Point Way by the flagpole and the memorial to World War II veterans. You are a block from the center here.

2. Captain Thomas Mellen House Main Street

The gray house on your left at the corner of Pease Point Way and Main Street was the home of Captain Mellen, master of the ship *Levi Starbuck,* which was captured and burned in the Civil War. He was also captain of the *Europa,* one of the ships that rescued 224 sailors in the Bering Sea in 1871. America's whaling fleet had become trapped in the ice, and it was thought the men would die from starvation and cold long before rescue vessels could reach them. Fortunately, ships were able to get through, thus avoiding what would have been the greatest disaster in America's whaling industry. This foursquare, nineteenth-century house with a columned doorway has had the front windows changed, but those on the back wing still have the twelve-over-twelve panes. It has a central hallway plan.

3. Dr. Daniel Fisher House Main Street

The next house on your left is Dr. Fisher's handsome transitional house, built in 1840, with the Greek Revival portico and intricately carved roof rail of the Federal period. The town's most successful and versatile businessperson at the time, Dr. Fisher supplied whale oil to many U.S. lighthouses. He also owned a large spermaceti candle factory on the waterfront, a hardtack bakery, and the town dock. He founded the Martha's Vineyard National Bank, operated a flour mill in North Tisbury, and practiced medicine! When it came to building his house, Dr. Fisher hired a Boston architect and insisted on the finest materials. It was framed with timbers of Maine pine that had been soaked in lime for two years and was constructed entirely with brass and copper nails. From

The Dr. Daniel Fisher House shows the delicate details of the Federal period and the Greek revival portico.

the enclosed cupola he could look far out to sea and observe the comings and goings of vessels during the height of the whaling era.

The richly carved balustrade around the roof and porch, as well as the beautiful portico, makes it one of the two most elegant structures in town. It is now owned by the Martha's Vineyard Preservation Trust. The trust was formed to save, restore, and make self-sufficient any important island buildings that might otherwise be sold for commercial purposes or radically remodeled. The Fisher house, one of six belonging to the trust, is beautifully decorated and open to the public for parties.

4. The Vincent House Main Street

On the spacious lawn behind the Fisher house is an old farmhouse also owned by the Martha's Vineyard Preservation Trust and open to the public. One of the oldest houses on the island (circa 1675), it was moved to its present site from the Great Plain area outside of Edgartown on the south shore. It's a fine example of a one-story full Cape, with two windows on either side of the front door, a huge central chimney with three fireplaces, and tiny stairs to the attic. The steep shed roof, flush with the windows, acts as both roof and wall, and the small ell was added at a later date. The house's present windows replaced the original diamond-shaped leaded lights. The changes and additions made to the house by various owners in the course of 300 years remain.

The building exemplifies for the public how these early houses were constructed; there are sections of wall left open and unfinished to show how the "wattle and daub" clay infilling was constructed. The house is open to the public in the summer.

5. The Old Whaling Church
Main Street

Continuing down Main Street, the next building on your left is the huge Methodist Church, more often called the Old Whaling Church, because it was built with whaling money in 1843. The lumber was brought down from Maine by Captain John Morse in his schooner. The magnificent organ was installed in 1869, and before the clock was built, there were four handsome Gothic windows. The church is the island's outstanding example of Greek Revival architecture. The enormous Gothic columns are its most distinctive feature, along with its 92-foot-high tower. The light in the steeple, once a beacon to sailors, can be seen by ships many miles at sea.

The church has long been an island landmark, but a rapidly diminishing Methodist congregation put the building's future in jeopardy until it was given to the Martha's Vineyard Preservation Trust. Funds were raised for its restoration, and it is now a performing arts center. Church services are held on Sundays during the summer months only.

6. St. Elizabeth's Church
Main Street

Diagonally across the street from the Old Whaling Church is the Catholic church. Although the Portuguese had been coming to the island from the Azores since Revolutionary times, Catholicism was not established here until much later.

The first Catholic church was built in Oak Bluffs in 1880, and St. Elizabeth's was built in 1925.

7. Dukes County Court House
Main Street

The next building on your left is the courthouse, built in 1858 and one of the first brick buildings constructed on the island. Originally the jailhouse was also here, but it was torn down in 1870, when the new jail and jailer's house were built farther up Main Street. All the county's business is conducted here, including sessions of the Superior Court each spring and fall.

8. Former Masonic Hall
School Street

Directly in front of the courthouse, across Main Street, take School Street. Just past the back of St. Elizabeth's Church, on your right, is a large columned building, the former Masonic Hall. It was built in 1839 as a Baptist church, but when the Baptists and Congregationalists united to form the Federated Church on South Summer Street, this building was taken over by the Masonic Lodge. It is now a private home.

9. Thaxter Academy
School Street

Continue down School Street and cross Davis Lane. Notice the handsome building on your right, at the corner. It was formerly a private school and is now a private home. It was built by Leavitt Thaxter, son of the minister of the Congregational Church, after he returned from sea and a teaching career in Massachusetts and Georgia. With his father's help, he built the academy. The classic form of the doorway is particularly handsome.

10. The Vineyard Museum
School and Cooke Streets

Continue on down School Street and at the corner you will see the grounds and buildings of the Vineyard Museum. This

Nancy Luce

Of all the museum's fascinating exhibits, those belonging to Nancy Luce are the most unusual. Luce was born in 1814 in West Tisbury. She became eccentric as she grew older. Nonetheless she supported herself knitting socks and mittens for whalemen, and later by selling her poems to tourists. It was her adored chickens, however, that fascinated everyone. And when a favorite hen died, she had the marble carver in Edgartown make a tombstone. These stones can be seen in the shed on the museum grounds, along with the 1854 Button hand-pump fire engine and other artifacts.

is the major historical center on the island; it houses the island's archives and many Colonial artifacts. It has more than one hundred whaling-vessel logbooks covering the period of the island's greatest prosperity from that industry.

The Thomas Cooke House was built in 1765 for Squire Cooke, a businessman, politician, justice, and collector of customs from 1784 through 1786. It is an exceptional example of a pre–Revolutionary War house, having had almost no modifications since the 1850s.

Out on the lawn is the magnificent, enormous Fresnel lens from the old Gay Head Lighthouse. Mounted in a replica of the watch room and lantern of the 1856 lighthouse, this French lens is a national treasure. One of very few extant, it is lit every night and is operated Sunday evenings in July and August, rotating as it originally did. There is an exhibition of its history in the watch room under the lens. Behind the light is a boat shed with some fascinating exhibits. The main building houses the Francis Foster Museum and the Gale Huntington Library of History. Next door the Captain Francis Pease house has an art gallery, displays of Indian artifacts, and other exhibits. All the buildings are open to the public. (See museums in chapter 9.)

Nancy Luce was famous for her chickens and homespun poetry. Her chickens' gravestones are at the Vineyard Museum.

11. Intersection of Cooke and School Streets

The three private houses opposite the entrance to the Vineyard Museum are fine examples of different types of architecture.

The small farmhouse, circa 1720, is typical of many early Vineyard houses and was moved by oxen to its present location. The large, handsome Captain Thomas Cooke House, across School Street, has two end chimneys and a central hall, which was popular in the late eighteenth century. Squire Cooke built this house for himself and gave his house on the museum grounds to his son at the time of his son's marriage. The small house diagonally across from the museum's entrance was built in 1820 by Captain Jethro Ripley, owner of a coasting schooner, who moved freight under sail for years.

12. First Federated Church
South Summer and Cooke Streets

Proceed down Cooke Street one block toward the waterfront to the corner of Cooke and South Summer Streets. The church here was originally built as a Congregational Church in 1828, but it merged with the Baptist Church a century later and became the Federated Church. It is a beautifully designed structure, and the interior contains old box pews as well as a Hook and Hastings organ. The chandelier has the original whale-oil lamps, and the church clock is one of the earliest bearing the name Ingraham. At night the light in the graceful and delicate steeple can be seen far out at sea. The parish house next door is an old schoolhouse that was moved here in 1850.

13. The Vineyard Gazette *Office*
South Summer Street

Continue on South Summer Street toward Main Street. At the corner of Davis Lane is the main office of the nationally known, award-winning weekly newspaper that has been in existence for 150 years. It is located in a house built by Captain Benjamin Smith in 1764. It was at one time a home for the poor, and the four rooms, each with a fireplace, accommodated four indigent families. A large addition has been constructed on the back of the building to accommodate the growing staff of the paper, while the interior of the original structure has been carefully preserved.

Henry Beetle Hough, the late author and editor, and his wife, Elizabeth Bowie Hough, owned and published the paper for forty-eight years, until Hough sold it to James Reston of the *New York Times* in 1968. His son, Richard Reston, is the editor and publisher. Hough continued writing the editorials until his death in 1984. Because of his lifelong crusade to preserve the natural beauty of the island, Hough was known as "the conscience of Martha's Vineyard."

The office of the Vineyard Gazette *is located in a pre-Revolutionary house on South Summer Street.*

14. Pagoda Tree South Water Street

Follow Davis Lane one block toward the waterfront to South Water Street. Turn left and head back toward Main Street, but as you do, be sure to notice the fine whaling captains' houses in this area. Their doorways, roof walks, and balustrades illustrate the Colonial, Federal, Greek Revival, and Victorian periods of architecture. In the middle of the block, on the right, is the huge Pagoda Tree. The tree was brought from China in a flowerpot by Captain Thomas Milton to plant beside his new home, now part of the Harborside Inn complex. Captain Milton first put in to Edgartown Harbor while serving aboard the privateer *Yankee* in the War of 1812. He liked the town so much that he bought this house lot in 1814 and some years later built the house at a cost of $900.

15. Town Dock and Chappaquiddick Ferry
Dock Street

At the corner of Main Street, turn right and head down toward the waterfront. The town parking lot and the Edgartown Yacht Club are straight ahead, but bear left along Dock Street. During the whaling era this was where the shops catering to the whaling industry were clustered together. Ship chandlers supplied whaleships tied up at the docks, where barrels of oil for Dr. Daniel Fisher's whale-oil factory were stacked.

Dr. Fisher also owned the town dock, now called Memorial Wharf. It is the termination point of the Memorial Day parade, where schoolchildren toss flowers into the harbor in memory of island residents who were lost at sea.

Beside the dock are the ferries to Chappaquiddick, called *On Time I, II,* and *III.* The first ferry was actually a rowboat, and freight was floated across on a barge.

16. Old Sculpin Art Gallery
Dock Street

Across from the town dock is the art gallery. This building was part of Dr. Daniel Fisher's whale-oil refinery and was later a feed mill. Its facade has not changed except for the small tower. In the early 1900s it became Manuel Swartz Roberts's boat shop, where he built catboats, which are small, gaff-rigged sailboats. They were beautifully constructed and became extremely popular. Summer visitors, island residents, and yacht sailors frequented his shop to admire the furniture and decoys he made as well as the boats.

The gallery is open all summer and shows the work of a series of interesting artists. The interior retains its old, weathered beams and uneven, pockmarked floor. The only modern addition is the pegboard on the walls, necessary for hanging paintings.

North Water Street

Walk up Daggett Street to the end and turn right on North Water Street. The Daggett House on this corner, built in

Historic North Water Street in Edgartown, which is lined with beautiful nineteenth-century houses built with whaling money.

1750, is the only pre-Revolutionary hip-roof house in the village. All along the street you will see some of the best examples of Colonial, Federal, and Greek Revival architecture on the island; many of them were built by shipwrights without the benefit of architects. These independent Yankees took all the liberties they liked with the prevailing styles, and modest adaptations of the purer forms are apparent in the roof, doorway, portico, window, and chimney arrangements.

Just past the Daggett House and across the street, three Colonial houses with Georgian adornments are set at a slight angle so the owners could see vessels rounding Cape Pogue on Chappaquiddick.

There are a number of very elegant houses with handsome facades along this street. Take time to walk slowly and study their architectural details. Number 68 North Water Street, built in 1784, has one of the handsomest doorways in town.

17. The John O. Morse House
Morse and North Water Streets

Just after you cross Morse Street, notice the large house on your left, the Morse House. It was built in 1840 at the height of the whaling era. Captain Morse owned a large commercial wharf down on the waterfront, just below the house, where the shipyard is now located. He was master of the whaleship *Hector,* known as "the luckiest whaleship afloat." Not only did he have "greasy luck," but he survived a battle with a sperm whale when the mammal took the captain's boat in his mouth, held it on end, and shook it to pieces. He survived, and from another whaleboat he buried his lance in the whale. During the height of the gold rush in 1849, he took time out from whaling to sail a group of men around the Horn to California in his bark, *Sarah.*

The original house had a porch on the first floor, looking seaward; the second-story porch was added at a later date. Some details on the facade reflect the earlier Federal period, while the heavy columns date to the Greek Revival period.

18. The Captain's House
North Water Street

As you continue on North Water Street, the next house on your left vies with the Dr. Daniel Fisher House as the most magnificent Federal mansion on the island, although they both have Greek Revival porticoes. Built in 1832 for Captain George Lawrence and sold, almost immediately, to Captain Jared Fisher, it represented the height of luxury for the time. It features Romanesque design with narrow sidelights, slender columns, gracefully carved balusters, and detailed trim on the roof walk, typical of the Federal period. Inside it has beautiful details on the ceilings, mantelpieces, and moldings.

Jared Fisher's granddaughter married into the Bliss family of Boston, and the house remained in the family for five generations before it was given to the Society for the Preservation

Painting the famous Edgartown Lighthouse

of New England Antiquities. It is not open to the public. Notice the mannequin of a woman on the roof walk, holding a spyglass and gazing out to sea over Chappaquiddick Island. It is a reminder of the women who searched for whaleships returning from the Pacific after several years' voyage.

19. The Lighthouse

Continuing along North Water Street, you pass by Cottage Street. It was in this area that Dr. Daniel Fisher had his spermaceti candle factory.

A little farther along you come to the path leading down to the automated lighthouse at the entrance to Edgartown Harbor and the beach. Where the lighthouse now stands, there was once a lighthouse keeper's house with a light tower on top. To reach it in those days, there was a long, wooden bridge over the marshy land to the beach. It was known as the "Bridge of Sighs," because young men used to take their dates for romantic evening strolls out to the beach.

Just up the street from the path, the house on your left next to the hotel has a Dutch gambrel roof, which is very rare in Vineyard architecture.

20. Emily Post House
Fuller Street

Continue past the hotel. From here the road curves around the bluff and is called Starbuck Neck. The houses fronting the outer harbor are typical, large, shingle-style, turn-of-the-century summer cottages. Starbuck Neck dead-ends at Fuller Street. Turn left here and head back toward the center of town. The second house on your right, past the two tennis courts, is the Emily Post House, with its beautiful garden. Considered the social arbiter of her day, Emily Post influenced the elite character of the town for years.

21. Saint Andrew's Episcopal Church
North Summer and Winter Streets

Continue straight ahead on Fuller Street to the end, turn right on Morse Street for half a block, and turn left onto North Summer Street. At the corner of Winter Street is the lovely, ivy-covered Episcopal Church. The cornerstone for the church was laid in 1899, and before that services were held in a room over a dry goods store on Main Street.

Diagonally across the street is a very fine example of an eighteenth-century half-Cape house; the dormers were a later addition. Across the street from the back of the church is one of the best examples of a Greek Revival house in Edgartown.

The late Henry Hough's family boathouse stands on the island's north shore, adjacent to Cedar Tree Neck.

At the end of the block, you are back on Main Street, and two blocks up to your right is where the tour began, at the corner of Pease Point Way.

22. Chappaquiddick Island

If you wish, return to the town dock, where you can take the ferry to Chappaquiddick.

It is difficult to see Chappy on foot unless you plan to take the whole day, because the main attraction is the beach on the far side of the island, 3 miles away. When you leave the ferry, stay on the hard-surfaced road past the private Chappaquiddick Beach Club on your left, and continue up the hill. The road meanders by scrub oak, pine, and masses of grapevines; it passes a gas station, the only commercial building on the island, and a new community center for island residents, then comes to a sharp right-hand curve. The road straight ahead leads to the Dyke Bridge and the Cape Pogue Wildlife Refuge; limited parking is available.

If you follow the paved road, it leads to Wasque Point, a wildlife reservation along the beach. There are signs directing the visitor to parking areas. Standing on this point, which is the southern tip of Chappaquiddick, and facing the sea, you can see the long sand spit on your right that connects the island with the Katama end of Edgartown at South Beach. Over the years the sea has broken through the barrier beach and separated the two islands during hurricanes or severe winter storms, and in time the ocean and currents build it up and close off the opening.

As you return to the ferry, you'll notice driveways leading to private homes. It wasn't until the middle of the eighteenth century that Chappaquiddick Island had any white settlers. Prior to that it was an Indian settlement and one of four sachemships (tribes) on Martha's Vineyard. In an Indian dialect Chappaquiddick meant "The Separated Island." When some of Edgartown's residents moved here, they engaged in shellfishing and raising corn, the island's principal livelihoods. Corn was exported to Maine and bartered for cedar posts to fence the cattle grazing on the open land. But the majority of residents were sea captains, and in 1878 a census listed forty-two—probably the highest number of sea captains in any community that size.

One resident, who was part owner of the island's corn gristmill, was also a patent-medicine king. Perry Davis started the manufacture of his Vegetable Pain Killer here. Its chief ingredients, however, were alcohol and opium, and it immediately became so successful that he moved his whole operation to Providence.

At one time there was a semaphore signal on Sampson's Hill, the highest point of land on the island. This was also where the Indians kept a lookout for whales and where the Humane Society boat was launched into the surf to go to the aid of vessels in distress on Muskeget Shoals. Before the Coast Guard began operating, there were lookouts fringing the island at strategic points, with the Humane Society's boats ready to be launched on a moment's notice.

The Chappaquiddick Indians were not treated well, and they were segregated in the North Neck area on poor land. Several Edgartownians tried to help them, but their help was late in coming; those who did survive poverty and the white settlers' diseases moved to Aquinnah or Cape Cod.

The famous old Alley's Store in the center of West Tisbury.

15

Up-Island Tour

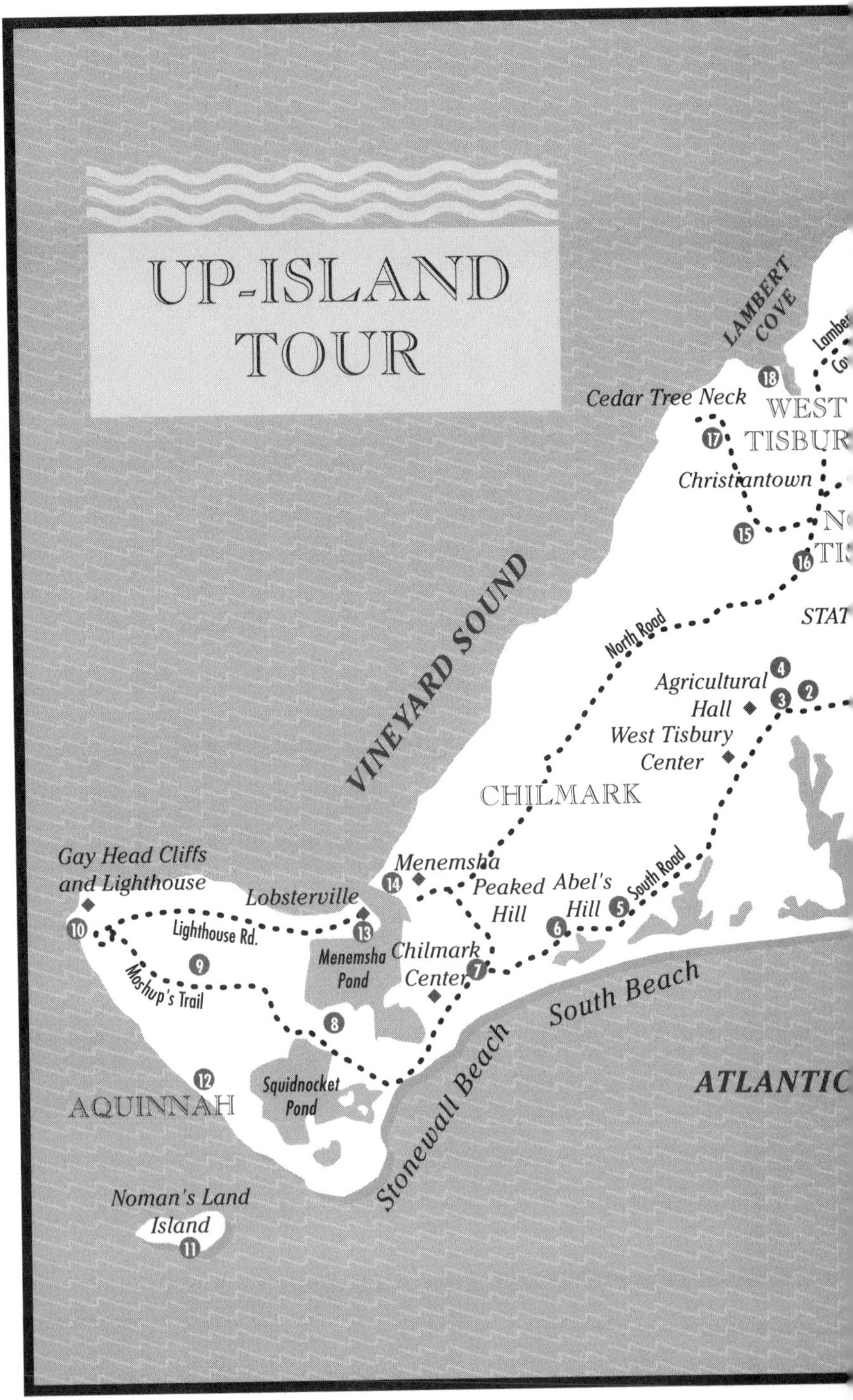

UP-ISLAND TOUR

LAMBERT COVE
Lambert's Cove
18
Cedar Tree Neck
WEST TISBURY
17
Christiantown
15
16
STATE
VINEYARD SOUND
North Road
4
Agricultural Hall
3
2
West Tisbury Center
CHILMARK
Gay Head Cliffs and Lighthouse
14
Menemsha
Peaked Hill
Abel's Hill
5
South Road
Lobsterville
10
Lighthouse Rd.
13
6
Menemsha Pond
Chilmark Center
7
9
Moshup's Trail
South Beach
8
12
AQUINNAH
Squidnocket Pond
Stonewall Beach
ATLANTIC
Noman's Land Island
11

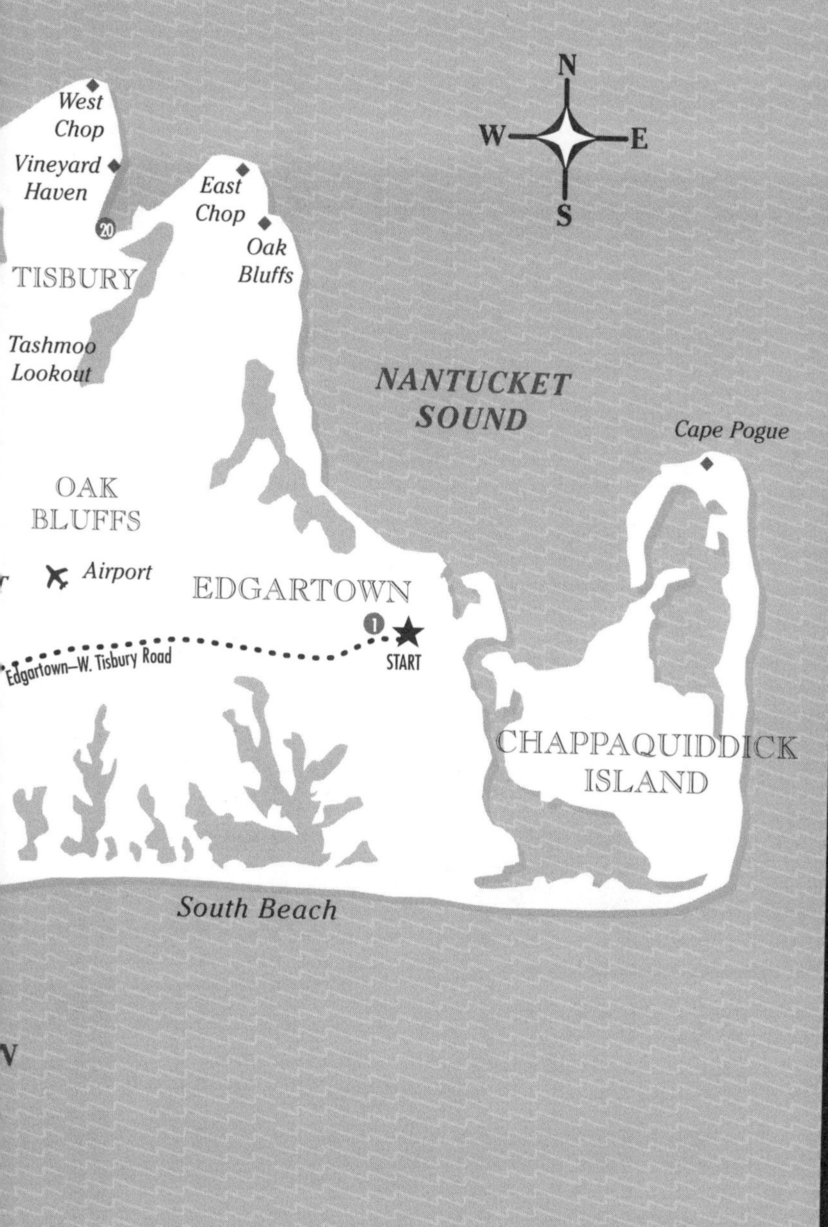
N
W
E
S
West Chop
Vineyard Haven
20
East Chop
Oak Bluffs
TISBURY
Tashmoo Lookout
NANTUCKET SOUND
Cape Pogue
OAK BLUFFS
Airport
EDGARTOWN
1
START
Edgartown–W. Tisbury Road
CHAPPAQUIDDICK ISLAND
South Beach

This Up-Island tour will take about two and a half hours, which includes stops of ten minutes or so at various places along the way.

1. Memorial Park

Begin at Memorial Park on upper Main Street on the outskirts of Edgartown, where the West Tisbury–Edgartown Road is clearly marked on the signs. This road was originally called the Takemmy Trail, and in the seventeenth century it led to an Indian village on the shores of Tisbury Great Pond near the ocean. The road is inland from the sea, and all the property on your left as you drive along is privately owned. About 2.5 miles out of Edgartown, on your right, is the beginning of the 4,000-acre state forest.

Four and a half miles from Edgartown, on the left, is the Place on the Wayside, a stone marker in memory of Thomas Mayhew, Jr., who often preached here to the Indians. The Indians placed stones on the spot in memory of young Mayhew, who was the most compassionate of all the Mayhews, and over the years added to the pile when they passed by to show their appreciation and affection. The stones have since been cemented together, and a bronze marker was erected by the Daughters of the American Revolution.

Continue past the airport and the youth hostel, on the outskirts of West Tisbury.

2. Mill Pond

At the Mill Pond the tiny building on your right was once a grammar school and later an icehouse. The mill itself dates back to the early part of the eighteenth century and was a fac-

The Mill Pond in West Tisbury is a fun place to feed the ducks and swans.

tory for the manufacture of satinet, a heavy fabric made from sheep's wool that was used for whaler's pea jackets. It is now the headquarters for the Martha's Vineyard Garden Club. The pond is a fun place for children to feed the ducks and swans.

3. West Tisbury Center

At the "T" intersection ahead, the road to your right leads past the West Tisbury cemetery to North Tisbury and back toward Vineyard Haven. Bear left to continue Up-Island along the shore on South Road. A charming, rural farming village in mid-island, West Tisbury was incorporated in 1671 and seems miles from the sea, but its boundaries cut a wide, north-south swath through the middle of the island. Horseback riding is very popular on the trails through woodlands, open fields, and alongshore. The old village store bears the advertisement "Dealers in Almost Everything." It is now owned by the Vineyard Preservation Trust. The handsome Congregational Church stands on the corner of Music Street, which got its name a hundred years ago when every house on the street was reputed to have a piano.

Across Music Street from the church, the small mansard-roofed building, formerly the library, is now the police department, and the building on the corner is the town hall. In the nineteenth century it was a coeducational school called the Dukes County Academy and was attended by local and mainland children. Whalers also attended classes here to brush up on schooling they'd missed because they went to sea at an early age.

4. Agricultural Society Barn

Turn right on Music Street, at the church, and keep to the right (do not take Middle Road). A short distance along is the Agricultural Hall, where the fair takes place, as well as other activities. This old barn, moved from New Hampshire and rebuilt with a great deal of volunteer help and contributions, is the pride of the island community. The spectacular concert given by James Taylor and Carly Simon, their first appearance together in sixteen years, was the highlight of 1995's fund raising for the barn.

The two-room Chilmark School in Beetlebung Corner, which was built in 1860.

5. Chilmark

Return to the church and bear right. A half-mile beyond West Tisbury's center is the town line of Chilmark. This is a town of hills, with stone walls rolling over the moors and reaching down to the sea, clumps of scrub oak and pine sculpted close to the ground by the relentless winds, wildflowers, and windswept beaches. Old Vineyard houses as well as very modern ones dot the landscape, and the spiky Scotch broom bursts into a brilliant yellow on the moors in June. Green ribbons of marsh fringe the tidal ponds, and from the high, rolling hills there are spectacular views of Vineyard Sound and the great sweep of the Atlantic Ocean.

Incorporated in 1694, and, like Tisbury, named for its parent town in England, Chilmark began as a fishing and farming community like other island villages. Great flocks of sheep roamed the moors, and the placement of houses reflected a feudal system of sheep farming on communally held property. Houses were sparsely scattered over the hillsides, unlike the Down-Island towns, where they were clustered together around the waterfront.

6. Abel's Hill

The South Road meanders along through the countryside, becoming hillier as it reaches a summit at Abel's Hill, named for an Indian whose wigwam once stood on this spot. The Chilmark cemetery has some unusual old gravestones and some famous new ones. Both comedian John Belushi and author Lillian Hellman are buried here. Up behind it is an Indian cemetery with fieldstones to mark the graves, the very small stones indicating children. While the cemetery can be visited, it is now against the law to make rubbings of these gravestones.

7. Chilmark Center

Two miles farther along, after passing over the little Fulling Mill Brook, which was once the site of a mill for thickening homemade woolen cloth, the road winds up a hill where open, rolling fields touch the sea. There is a dirt road on the left that leads to the Lucy Vincent Beach, which is for Chilmark residents and guests only. Just before this road, on the right, there's an old full-Cape house framed with a magnificent stone wall, which has its place in Up-Island history.

Called Barn House, it was started in 1920 as a private inn. The main house was used for meals. The chicken coops and outbuildings were converted into living quarters, and the large barn was fixed up for social gatherings. Barn House was organized by a group of extreme liberals, some of Marxist and Communist persuasion, who summered here with their families. In the ensuing years such well-known figures as the Socialist Norman Thomas; Roger Baldwin, the founder of the American Civil Liberties Union; Felix Frankfurter, who went on to become a Supreme Court justice; and the journalist Walter Lippmann visited with Barn House's founder, Stanley King, who was president of Amherst College at the time. The Vineyarders called Barn House "that hangout for radicals."

There were others in the arts who came here in the twenties and thirties, not only because they preferred Chilmark's sparsely settled, rural character, but also because it was often all they could afford. A fish house or barn might be rented for the summer for $25. The informality and social gatherings,

Writers' Retreat

By the 1920s many intellectuals and writers began spending their summers Up-Island. Many came here because the rentals were so inexpensive, while others preferred the quiet, isolated areas where they could work without interruptions. They often did find time to go Down-Island to give lectures, which were, and still are, most interesting as noted by the local paper.

"Nobel Prize winner and long time Chilmark summer resident Robert Solow promised his audience a question and answer period after his talk at the Nathan Mayhew Seminars. But he instructed them not to ask whether interest rates would rise in the next six months. 'If I knew, I would have a much fancier house than I have,' he remarked."

Courtesy, *Vineyard Gazette,* Copyright May 12, 1988

which in those days included summer and year-round residents, appealed to people in the arts.

Just before the intersection, which is the center of Chilmark, is the Community Center on your left, which is the gathering place for Chilmark residents. This intersection was named Beetlebung Corner for the grove of Beetlebung trees (a local term for tupelos) on your right, which are enclosed with a split-rail fence. The wood from these oriental-looking trees, whose leaves turn a fiery red in the fall, is extremely tough, and for years it was used to make wooden mallets (beetles) and bungs to plug the bungholes of wooden casks and barrels.

Chilmark Center has a two-room schoolhouse that looks the same as it did in 1860, when it was illustrated in *Harper's* magazine. The town hall, firehouse, several stores, and delicately spired Methodist Church complete this rural village. In 1828 this church was moved from Edgartown to the Middle Road, and in 1915 to its present location, where Roger Allen, a highly respected town official who was a superb carpenter, built the steeple.

8. On the Road to Gay Head (now called Aquinnah)

Three roads converge at the center of Chilmark: Middle Road, to your right, goes back to Music Street in West Tisbury; Menemsha Cross Road, straight ahead, goes to Chilmark's port; and the South Road, to your left, continues on to Aquinnah.

Bear left on the South Road. A mile farther along, there's a bridge, the only link to this end of the island. There is a boat ramp on your right into Nashaquitsa Pond, and Stonewall Pond is on the left. A tenth of a mile beyond, the stone enclosure on the left is an old cattle pound that was used for stray cows and sheep when thousands roamed the moors.

The road winds up a hill to the lookout, which affords a spectacular view of Nashaquitsa and Menemsha Ponds, dotted with white sails, and hillside farmhouses weathered to a silvery gray. Beyond the ponds is Menemsha, and across Vineyard Sound the Elizabeth Islands stand out on a clear day.

The hilly road winds around the Aquinnah town line at Herring Creek. In the eighteenth and nineteenth centuries, herring was very important to the island's economy. The fish were seined out of many island creeks when they swam up into ponds in the spring to spawn. They were pickled in barrels for export, salted, smoked, or used for cod and lobster bait. Later the scales were sold for making "Priscilla pearls."

At the creek the small, gray house fronting on Menemsha Pond, to your right, belonged to the Missouri artist Thomas Hart Benton, who was renowned for his many murals, including one in the Truman Library. The Bentons summered on the island for fifty-five years.

9. Aquinnah

Continue straight on the South Road to the Gay Head Cliffs. Aquinnah is as famous for its cliffs, now a National Landmark, as it is for its people. Both are deserving of their place in history. Aquinnah is one of the two Indian townships in the state of Massachusetts (Mashpee is the other). The town was incorporated in 1870, and the Indians were merged in the general community with all the "rights and privileges and with all the duties and liabilities of citizens."

Prior to then the town was part of Chilmark. The Indians had always willingly shared their knowledge of fishing and planting crops, including the way to steam fish and shellfish on a beach (the origin of the clambake). In turn, the white settlers' efforts to Christianize and educate the Indians were well rewarded when one Aquinnah Indian went to Harvard as early as 1665, and another served in the state legislature in the nineteenth century. The Indians lived in loosely constructed wigwams covered with mats woven of marsh grasses. They moved from place to place, not only to let the soil rest, but also to take advantage of coastal and inland climates. They lived alongshore in warmer months and moved back into the woods and valleys in winter.

The Indians were extremely able, courageous sailors, and because it was considered good luck to have an Indian aboard, they were in great demand as helmsmen on whaleships. It was the coxswain in the longboat who cast the first iron into the whale. They attained immortality as whalers through Tashtego, the Gay Head Indian in Herman Melville's classic, *Moby-Dick.* Another who gained local renown was Amos Smalley, the only Vineyarder known to have harpooned

Gay Head Lighthouse

During the summer, the Gay Head Lighthouse is open to the public on weekends, and the view of the surrounding sea and sunsets is spectacular. The iron spiral stairway ascends to a brownstone walkway circling the tower. The final ascent is up a steep ladder to the glass room housing the rotating beacon. Admission is $2.00 for adults, and children under twelve are free.

a white whale. Melville referred to the town Gay Head and the name was changed to Aquinnah in June 1998.

A cluster of houses alongside the main road, before you reach the cliffs, is the village center; the former one-room schoolhouse on the left is now the town library. The road beside the library leads to a very beautiful Baptist church in a setting of rolling fields and gray stone walls, high over the Atlantic Ocean. Dating to the seventeenth century, it is the oldest Indian Baptist church in North America. The town's police department and town hall are across from the library on the main road.

10. Gay Head Cliffs and Lighthouse

There are ample parking areas and gift and food shops at the cliffs, which are one of the island's great scenic attractions. Named by British sailors in the seventeenth century for their brilliant colors, the cliffs were often mentioned in logs and journals. They were a landmark to sailors outward bound on voyages that sometimes lasted years, and for those returning to New Bedford or the Vineyard, they were the first sight of home. The twisted strata of these multicolored cliffs, which are of particular interest to geologists and paleontologists, recount millions of years of the earth's formation. Years ago the Indians dug clay out of the cliffs, to be shipped to mainland potteries on coastal schooners. Facing west from the lookout, the Elizabeth Islands, on your right, extend in a chain from Woods Hole, and the small deserted island of Noman's Land is to your left.

The Gay Head Cliffs are a premier tourist attraction on the island.

As early as 1799 there was a tended lighthouse on this point to mark the entrance to Vineyard Sound and to warn ships away from the great reef of glacial boulders extending out from the cliffs for almost a mile. It was here on the night of January 18, 1884, that the worst shipwreck in Martha's Vineyard history occurred when the ironhulled steamship *The City of Columbus* struck the rocks. En route from Boston to Savannah on a bright moonlit night, with heavy seas running and high winds, the vessel struck the ledge about 3:00 A.M. It was five hours before a Humane Society boat was able to reach the vessel, where survivors clung to the icy rigging in the frigid blackness, praying and waiting for dawn. The strength of 122 passengers, one after another, gave out, and they dropped into the sea. The heroic efforts of the islanders who rowed through mountainous waves to rescue survivors is another memorable episode in the history of Aquinnah's mariners.

The original lighthouse here was one of the first revolving ones in the country; often the wooden works became swollen in damp weather, and the keeper or his wife was obliged to turn the light by hand all night long. In 1856 this was replaced by a larger steel structure that housed a stronger light with a Fresnel lens. In 1952 the present automatic light was erected, and the old lens was given to the Vineyard Museum.

11. Noman's Land Island

Standing on the cliffs, facing west, Noman's is the island on your left. Although there have been many theories, the origin of the name of Noman's Land is unknown. In the nineteenth century this was a fishing outpost for Vineyarders, who built fish houses on the north side of the island and spent half the year here, cod fishing in spring and fall and lobstering in summer. Some brought their families with them, others went back and forth to the Vineyard, and a few families lived here year-round, fishing and raising sheep. In the late 1800s as many as sixty boats worked out of Noman's Land. It is now owned by the U.S. government and will become a wildlife preserve. The islands on your right are the Elizabeth Islands.

12. Moshup's Trail

Facing Down-Island from the cliffs, Moshup's Trail is to your right. The road loops down along the Aquinnah beach and then connects back to the South Road. The Indians called Gay Head *Aquinnah,* meaning "Long End" or "Point," and Moshup's Trail is named for a legendary giant and hero of both the Vineyard and Cape Cod Indians. Among the many stories about his extraordinary abilities is one about the boulders at Devil's Bridge, which he is supposed to have put down so he could walk over to Cuttyhunk at the tip of the Elizabeth Islands; as the legend goes, he abandoned the idea before it was completed. He is also said to have dragged his toe over a barrier beach that connected Noman's Land and the Vineyard, causing the beach to disappear with the first high tide. His most famous feat, according to Indian lore, was to knock the ashes out of his pipe while fishing off Chappaquiddick, thereby making Nantucket.

13. Lobsterville

Again facing Down-Island from the cliffs, go left on Lighthouse Road, which makes a loop down along Vineyard Sound to Lobsterville. This was the island's most important fishing village in the nineteenth century, before the creek leading into Menemsha Pond was dredged and riprapped in 1905 to make Menemsha Harbor. The cluster of net houses and fish houses used by lobstermen, trap fishermen, and hand-liners in the days when smacks arrived from New York to buy lobsters for five cents apiece is gone. It is a fine beach for swimming and fishing. (Parking is limited for both residents and nonresidents.) The Cranberry Lands across the road is a nesting site for thousands of gulls in the early spring and a favorite spot for bird watchers. There is no trespassing allowed on these beautiful, low, rolling moors covered with wild roses, bayberry, dusty miller, and cranberries.

At the end of the Lobsterville Road is a boat ramp, and just across the creek is Menemsha. To get there, retrace your steps back to Lighthouse Road and South Road, and go left to Beetlebung Corner.

14. Menemsha

At the intersection the road straight ahead is the Middle Road, which goes straight back to West Tisbury. There are no historic sites on the road, but there are several wildlife sanctuaries. For this tour, bear left at the corner and take the Menemsha Cross Road, which leads down to Chilmark's port, considered to be the last true fishing village on the island. The large number of pleasure boats tied up here each summer has somewhat changed the character of the port, however.

Menemsha has its own post office in the general store, and the fishermen's colorful boathouses lining the west side of the basin have been a favorite subject of artists for years. The island's Coast Guard station is located here, and their vessels are kept on this side of the harbor; the commercial fishing boats tie up along Dutcher's Dock on the east side of the basin. Menemsha now has a marina with plug-ins, and tourism dominates the local economy.

Menemsha Bight, just offshore, and the sea around Noman's Land have always been popular sport-fishing areas, and charter boats go out from here to the fishing grounds. The beach is open to the public.

For bikers pedaling to Aquinnah, there is a little bike ferry here. This quick crossing to the flat Lobsterville Road avoids the very steep hills to Aquinnah and ends at the cliffs.

Menemsha

Menemsha is at its best in the off-season: The storekeepers and fishermen have time to hang around Squid Row, a marvelous wooden bench on the pier where they discuss town affairs. There's even plenty of time in the late fall or very early spring for backgammon in the general store and post office.

In the 1920s writers, college presidents, and artists such as Thomas Hart Benton and Vaclav Vytlacil, were among those who found the simple, cheap rentals and primitive conditions of Menemsha appealing. They walked everywhere along the winding dirt roads, got their fish when the boats came in, and went skinny dipping at Roger Baldwin's place on the south shore.

15. North Tisbury

Leaving Menemsha, take the North Road to North Tisbury. There are no easily identifiable historic sites along this wooded, winding road, which, like the South Road, is inland from the sea. The dirt driveways you see along the way lead to private houses whose occupants value their privacy and the seclusion of the North Shore. There are several wildlife sanctuaries off the North Road.

On the right you will pass the sign for Tea Lane, which dates back to Revolutionary times, when no true patriot would drink tea that had been taxed by England but would smuggle it in "duty free." A Captain Robert Hillman sneaked some tea home from England for a sick relative and gave the little dirt road its name.

There are several brooks along the North Road that run down from the Chilmark hills into Vineyard Sound. Years ago they provided sites for a brickyard, where Vineyard clay was used to make bricks for local consumption as well as export, a paint mill, and several gristmills.

Some of the island's famous sea captains came from the North Shore area, including Captain George Fred Tilton and his brother, Captain Zeb Tilton. The former gained renown for his 2,000-mile trek down the coast of Alaska to get help when America's whaling fleet was caught in the ice at Point Barrow in 1897. Zeb, a legendary coastal schooner captain who owned the *Alice S. Wentworth,* was known from Boston to Brooklyn for his wit, skill, and attraction for women during the sixty years he moved freight under canvas.

At a fork in the road, bear left beside the magnificent oak tree with huge branches curving down to the ground. You are in the center of North Tisbury, although, increasingly, people are calling it West Tisbury, which can be a little confusing. At one time the town was an agricultural community. Here were a church, schoolhouse, blacksmith, and general store, where for years the stage from Vineyard Haven changed horses. All have disappeared, but the town has retained its rural charm; there are some interesting old houses and several stores well worth seeing. Stop at the Vineyard Food Shop—known as Humphrey's—an island institution, where delicious baked goods, seasonal jellies and jams, and beverages are for sale.

16. The Polly Hill Arboretum

Bear right at the intersection of North Road and State Road and a quarter mile along is the beautiful arboretum.

It was more than forty years ago that Polly Hill and her husband began to spend the summer at a farm called Barnard's Inn in North Tisbury. An amateur gardener, she began planting all sorts of seeds, trees, shrubs, and flowers at their new summer home—magnolias and camelias thrived in this climate along with 2,000 other plants. Through the years Polly has developed new strains of plants, which are sold in national catalogs. She is recognized internationally for her work.

Today the sixty acre arboretum is open to the public year-round. It has a visitor's center and a barn for educational and special events. Closed Wednesdays. Admission is $5.00 for adults and $3.00 for children under twelve. For more information call 693–0925.

Return to the intersection by the oak tree and Humphrey's Bakery.

17. Christiantown

A half-mile along State Road, on your left, is the sign for Indian Hill Road. This leads to a crossroads and a sign pointing straight ahead down a dirt road to the Indian graveyard and chapel at Christiantown, which is a half-mile farther. This ancient township was started in 1659 with a grant of 1 square mile given by Sachem Josias Keteanummin of Takemmy as a new home for Indian converts to Christianity. A plaque on a boulder commemorates "the services of Governor Thomas Mayhew and his descendant missionaries who here labored among the native Indians."

The Christiantown Meeting House, or chapel, was erected in 1829. It is a fascinating little building surrounded by a wildflower garden, and inside there are a tiny altar and six pews on either side of the aisle. The nearby fieldstones mark the old Indian gravesites.

Behind the Indian graveyard a footpath leads through the woods to the fire tower lookout, which commands a view of the surrounding countryside.

18. Cedar Tree Neck Wildlife Sanctuary

Retrace your steps to the hard-surfaced road. A right turn on Indian Hill Road goes to the Cedar Tree Neck Wildlife Sanctuary. There are several old Cape houses in this rural setting that are unspoiled by development; they show what these self-sufficient island communities looked like a hundred years ago.

The road climbs to a sharp curve where a sign points the way down a very narrow, bumpy dirt road for a mile to the 250-acre wildlife sanctuary. It is maintained as a "natural habitat for wildlife and as a living museum for the enjoyment of all who love the outdoors and wish to follow the marked trails through the woods and along the beach and to look out from the height of Cedar Tree Neck." With its herring pond, meadows, rocky bluffs, woodland of scrub oak and beech trees, bayberry, and freshwater stream flowing into the sea, this unusually varied terrain exemplifies the character of the island's north shore.

19. Lambert's Cove

Return to the State Road and bear left toward Vineyard Haven. A short distance ahead on the left is Lambert's Cove Road. Inland from the sea, with woods and hills to preclude any view of the water, it is a pretty drive through the countryside, but there are few historic sites visible from the road. Lambert's Cove was once a sizable fishing and farming community with its own ferry running to Woods Hole. A short distance in from the highway on the right is Uncle Seth's Pond, now a favorite place for ice skating. Farther along you'll pass the Methodist Church, which originated in 1846, and its lovely old hillside cemetery. Alongshore in this area there was once a brick works that produced both red and yellow brick from island clay.

20. Tashmoo Lookout

Lambert's Cove Road dead-ends back on the State Road by the lovely Tashmoo Farm, with its magnificent stone walls and rolling pastures. Bear left, and just ahead on the left is Tashmoo Lookout, which affords a lovely view across Vineyard Sound to the Elizabeth Islands. In Indian dialect *tashmoo* means "at the great spring." The opening to the sound was originally a creek where anglers used to seine for herring in the spring. It wasn't until the present century that the opening was dredged and riprapped to enable boats to enter what is now known as Lake Tashmoo.

A short distance ahead is the center of Vineyard Haven, the end of this tour.

Epilogue

The fascination of an island resort is that it provides an escape from urban America; it also offers the seclusion, simplicity, easy point of reference, and strong identity of small-town America. On the Vineyard the magical attraction is not only the individuality of the six towns—the historic villages, the galaxy of entertainment in the Down-Island towns, and the bucolic Up-Island farms—but the variety and scope of the island's natural beauty: the timeless lure of the restless sea framing the broad, windswept beaches; brilliant skies; thick woodlands of scrub oak and pine; freshwater ponds and streams; high, rolling hills reminiscent of Scottish moors; excellent offshore sailing; and harbors teeming with the graceful movement of ships.

The soaring popularity of the island has been both a blessing and a curse. The Vineyard is very fragile, after all, and the delicate balance between people and nature—so necessary for the island to retain its character—is constantly being challenged. Overdevelopment in many areas is threatening this balance, and growth, often without planning, has been the source of endless controversy. It has jeopardized the water table, wildlife, wetlands, harbors, and shellfish industry. Most important of all, the island risks losing its innate personality, that unique quality that offshore islands acquire over the centuries. The great interest in America's heritage has increased dramatically since the Bicentennial, especially on the Vineyard, where the thread of history winds through the island like gossamer. Its historic roots and wildlife preserves are the island's most valuable assets.

Fortunately, many dedicated individuals, both summer and island residents, have had the foresight and appreciation of history to understand the problem. They have worked long and hard to set aside wildlife areas and preserve historic buildings, aware that overdevelopment would not only damage the natural environment, but also change the face of the island in an irreversible manner.

Toward this end there are six organizations working to preserve, protect, and acquire properties to help maintain the balance. Currently about 20 percent of the island's landmass, including wetlands, farmland, beaches, and wildlife areas, is protected from any commercial development, and the work goes on. While the island has been settled for 350 years, it belongs to nature and to history, and its future depends on how citizens and visitors treat this beautiful, but very fragile, outpost.

INDEX

A

B

C

D

E

F

G

H

I

N

O

P

Q

R

S

T

U

V

W

Y

Z

About the Author

Polly Burroughs has been a resident of Martha's Vineyard for many years, both in summer and now year-round. She has written thirteen previous books, including Globe Pequot's *Guide to Nantucket, Zeb: A Celebrated Schooner Life, The Great Ice Ship Bear, Thomas Hart Benton: A Portrait, Eisenstaedt: Martha's Vineyard, Martha's Vineyard Houses and Gardens,* and *Alaska: 1889,* with George B. Grinnell.

When she's not writing, Mrs. Burroughs enjoys such island activities as tennis, swimming, and gardening.

About the Photographer

Mike Wallo, a professional photographer for fifteen years, is also the Production Manager of the *Vineyard Gazette.* Originally from New Jersey, he attended Rutgers University and worked for a number of New Jersey daily newspapers before joining the *Gazette* staff in 1980. He and his wife, Susan, and their daughter live in Oak Bluffs.

Most of the photographs shown here have been previously published in the *Vineyard Gazette.*